The Book That America's Business Leaders Are Talking About:

ON MY HONOR, I WILL

more ...

"ON MY HONOR, I WILL is bursting with down-to-earth stories and reflections on the importance of strong moral character in the practice of business."

—Gary E. Edwards, president, Ethics Resource Center, Inc.

→

"A straight-shooting book."

—*Success* magazine

→

"Will help us...breed success in our businesses, our community and in our personal lives."

—Edwin M. Cooperman, chairman and co-CEO, American Express Travel Related Services Co., Inc.

→

"ON MY HONOR is just the prescription for our rapidly declining moral values. Pennington and Bockmon have done yeoman's work to make their case."

—Walter Williams, Distinguished Professor of Economics at George Mason University and syndicated newspaper columnist

→

"ON MY HONOR may help many troubled decision-makers rethink and apply to their work and their companies the simple morality they learned as children."

—Robert L. Dilenschneider, former president and CEO, Hill and Knowlton

→

"While people 'scout for answers,' this book provides a refresher course on values/behaviors desperately needed in today's business world."

—Susan RoAne, bestselling author of *How to Work a Room*

→

ON MY HONOR, I WILL

HOW ONE SIMPLE OATH CAN LEAD YOU TO SUCCESS IN BUSINESS

RANDY PENNINGTON AND MARC BOCKMON
FOREWORD BY ZIG ZIGLAR

WARNER BOOKS

A Time Warner Company

Warner Books, Inc., 1271 Avenue of the Americas, New York, NY 10020

 A Time Warner Company

Printed in the United States of America

First trade printing: June 1993

10 9 8 7 6 5 4 3 2 1

Library of Congress Cataloging-in-Publication Data

Pennington, Randy.
    On my honor, I will : how one simple oath can lead you to success in business / by Randy Pennington and Marc Bockmon.
        p.   cm.
    ISBN 0-446-39495-5
    1. Leadership—Moral and ethical aspects.   2. Business ethics.
I. Bockmon, Marc, 1943–   .   II. Title.
HD57.7.P45   1992
174'.4—dc20   91-50400
                                                                      CIP

Book design by Giorgetta Bell McRee
Cover design by Anthony Russo
Cover photograph by Fotografica of New York

To Mary, my partner in love and life.
RANDY PENNINGTON

*To Marie, the woman of honor who
became my wife.*
MARC BOCKMON

ACKNOWLEDGMENTS

We wish to acknowledge and say "thank you" to the following people and organizations for their assistance and encouragement. Without them, this project would not have been as enjoyable or successful.

- Lloyd Jones, our literary agent, for his hard work and willingness to take a chance.
- Joann Davis, Executive Editor at Warner Books, for her enthusiasm and good ideas. She made this a better book and destroyed every negative stereotype we ever heard about editors.
- William C. Gamble of the Boy Scouts of America Circle Ten Council for his support and ability to get things done.

- Ray Robbins, Roger Staubach, John P. Hayes, and Zig Ziglar for giving their support early in the project and continuing it to the end.
- Susan Clay, Pearle, Inc.; Dave Chase, Lennox International; Allan Cecil, National Gypsum Corp.; Liz Barrett, Mary Kay Cosmetics; Duncan Muir, JCPenney; and the other corporate public relations professionals and executive assistants who helped us get to the right people and receive the right information.
- Steve Ventura for helping us brainstorm many of the ideas for the project.
- Eric Harvey, Al Lucia, and the staff at Performance Systems Corporation in Dallas for their friendship, support, encouragement and influence.
- Howard Putnam for providing a living example of high integrity, leadership and professionalism to strive toward.
- Dennis and Niki McCuistion, Jim Patrick, and Valerie Sokolosky, who kept encouraging.
- The organizations and individuals discussed in the book and contributing with endorsements. They prove every day that integrity and success are related.

THE SCOUT OATH

On my honor, I will do my best:
1. To do my duty to God and my country, and to obey the Scout Law;
2. To help other people at all times;
3. To keep myself physically strong, mentally awake, and morally straight.

"The central need of our times is to find the road we lost or abandoned, and to recover the values we have rejected in favor of every man for himself in pursuit of egoistic goals."

—LASLO NAGY
Secretary-General
World Organization of the Scout Movement

CONTENTS

FOREWORD

There's a persistent belief that "nice guys finish last." Not only do they not finish last, but they ultimately finish at or near the top, while the "bad guys" consistently finish behind the eight-ball, behind bars, or near the bottom. *On My Honor* by Randy Pennington and Marc Bockmon gives some magnificent insights and instructions that will help make you a winner in your personal, family, and business life. Here is an on-target, up-to-date, common-sense approach to why we must be teaching principles, procedures, and values that worked in the beginning of our country's history and will work even better today.

In this day and age when many facets of our society

are coming apart at the seams, it's refreshing and exciting to read a book based on the principles taught in the Boy Scout organization. In this day of drive-by shootings, x-rated "entertainment," drug and alcohol problems, teenage pregnancies, crime, theft and violence, it's refreshing to have authors who boldly advocate the principles of pledging, "On my honor I will do my best." When we adopt the principles of "honor and best effort," we're building a solid foundation for success. When we include courtesy, kindness, obedience, cheerfulness, and friendliness, we describe an individual who will be a success in his personal, business, social, and family life.

When a scout (or you) pledges to do his duty to God and country and to keep himself morally straight and physically clean, he moves out of the crowd at the bottom and starts climbing toward the top. When a person agrees to be trustworthy, think of what that means in a society where, according to a recent bestseller, 91 percent of the people in America will indiscriminately lie about a host of things.

What's exciting about the principles espoused in *On My Honor* is the fact that they work in every facet of our lives. Question: Did you ever wonder why in the 1770s three million Americans produced Thomas Jefferson, Benjamin Franklin, George Washington, John Adams, James Monroe, James Madison, and a host of other truly brilliant leaders, and in 1990 250 million Americans produced _____? (I believe you would be hard-pressed to find even one name you would be willing to list as having the greatness of the men listed above.)

Could it be that what those early Americans were taught had a direct bearing on their performance and accomplishments? For example, according to the Thomas

Jefferson Research Institute, in the 1770s over 90 percent of our educational thrust was aimed at teaching moral values. At that time most of the education was handled in the home, church, or in church-supported schools. By 1926 the percentage of moral training had reduced to 6 percent, and by 1951 the percentage was so low you could not even measure it.

Now tie this to the fact that according to a May, 1989, issue of *Psychology Today*, reporting on a study of 1,139 chief executive officers who had an average salary of $356,000, their number-one asset was their integrity and their number-one priority was their family. Now combine this with the April 28, 1986, issue of *Fortune* magazine, where we learn that 91 percent of the CEOs of the Fortune 500 companies are people of faith, which means they probably received their moral and values training at home, in a house of worship. In short, the truly successful people in all areas of their lives build their careers on a solid ethical base.

In this easy-to-read example-filled book, Randy Pennington and Marc Bockmon give example after example right out of today's society of men and women who have applied the principles they talk about in the book and achieved remarkable results. I enthusiastically endorse *On My Honor* for one very simple reason: These gentlemen are espousing principles that work— that worked yesterday, work today, and will work tomorrow, perhaps even better. Tom Peters expressed it well when he said integrity always has been and always will be the key to successful accomplishment. You will both enjoy and benefit from *On My Honor.*

—Zig Ziglar

CHAPTER ONE

ONCE UPON
A BUSINESS TRIP

2:25 P.M. We were at an impasse. Mr. Horton[1] had
hired us to provide consultation services for his firm.
The project had gone well and everyone was pleased.
In fact, after the project had begun, Mr. Horton
agreed to extend the scope of the agreement for an
extra fee.

Now, he was claiming he had always believed the
extra work had been part of the original package and
denied agreeing to any additional charges.

We *knew* we were right, and Mr. Horton *said* he was
right. The old saying "An unwritten agreement isn't
worth the paper it's written on" came to mind. Obvi-

[1]Not his real name.

1

ously, without written evidence or corroborating testi-mony, judgment defaulted to Horton's firm.

"What about Mike Johnson[2]?" I asked, remembering that Horton's vice president of finance had attended the meeting where the extra work was discussed, priced, and approved.

The client gave us a "now-I've-got-you" smile and picked up the phone. He buzzed his superior and asked him to join us. When Mr. Johnson arrived, Horton gave him the details of the dispute, making his own position perfectly clear.

Johnson listened carefully until his associate fin-ished, then shook his head. "Oh, no! They told us about the extra charge up front and we both agreed it was fair! Don't you remember? *In fact, you said the price was more than fair!*"

Horton mumbled something, thanking his supervi-sor. After Johnson left, Horton began shuffling papers on his desk. The somewhat awkward silence was bro-ken by my associate who said with relief, "I'm glad Mr. Johnson remembered."

Horton shook his head in disgust. "Yeah, he's a real Boy Scout."

4:00 P.M. As we drove back to the airport we began to wonder about Horton's disparaging remark that Johnson was a "real Boy Scout." The implication was that any-one who valued integrity more than money had some-what defective judgment.

And what about Horton? Had he fallen into the mind trap of believing greed was good? That the end justified the means? That honor and integrity belonged to another era? That Boy Scout principles were ar-

[2]Not his name either.

chaic, outmoded, and fit only for children? If so, a quick scan of recent headlines about the arrest of traitors, swindlers, confidence men, crooked stockbrokers, S&L executives, etc., would indicate he was not alone. It was almost as if there had been a shift in moral values. If so, it might explain the apparent moral malaise in American business.

We were not the only ones to notice that American business had a problem. A rash of pop-management books has sought to offer quick-fix solutions by concentrating on the basics of business. The problem is, quick-fix solutions are often more quick than fix. Besides, quick fixes, like quick-fix diets, usually don't last, because it takes time to change your way of eating—or living.

The search for solutions had birthed so many books that one client defined the phenomenon as "management by best-seller." In our frantic search to find quick cures, we are in danger of becoming a nation of Ponce de Leóns, seeking a magic spring that would restore youthful vitality to our careers and our businesses.

It isn't so much that such books aren't helpful—most are. It is just that we can't bring about *internal change* with *external medicine*. To change our work and our workplace, the change must come from within. Changing from within takes more time and effort, but it brings lasting change. It's the kind of change that shifts the focus from *who is right* to *what is right*. Then and only then can we be truly successful.

4:20 P.M. We arrived at the airport, checked our luggage, then ordered coffee in the terminal restaurant. My colleague, obviously still bothered by Horton's remark, sighed and asked me what the phrase "a real Boy Scout" meant to me.

"One who lives by the Scout Oath," I replied. "Remember it?"

Somewhat to the amazement of the waitress, who had arrived with coffee, we recited the oath together.

"On my honor, I will do my best:
To do my duty to God and my country, and to obey the Scout Law.
To help other people at all times,
To keep myself physically strong, mentally awake, and morally straight."

We moved on to recite the Scout Law:

"A scout is trustworthy, loyal, helpful, friendly, courteous, kind, obedient, cheerful, thrifty, brave, clean, and reverent."

The waitress departed with a puzzled look on her face. My friend remarked, "These are admirable qualities. Why did Horton use the term 'Boy Scout' as if it were a derogatory term? Isn't it a *compliment*? Wouldn't we want 'Boy Scouts' and 'Girl Scouts' for employees? For customers? For suppliers? For supervisors and managers?"

I had to admit these were good questions, and the answers seemed obvious. After all, it *was the Scout Oath and the Scout Law that first caused business people to devote their time, talent, and financial resources to the movement!* These early Scouting pioneers recognized that the virtues that made good Scouts also made good citizens, good customers, good competitors, and good employees.

Consequently, it's not surprising that Scouting is best known for character building. Character building was a major goal of the Scouting movement from the beginning, back in 1907 when British general Sir Robert Baden-Powell, a war hero who achieved national prominence, organized a camp for twenty boys. A year later, he published his Boy Scout manual, and the movement swept England. In his book, *Scouting for Boys,* Baden-Powell proclaimed, "Scouting is a school of citizenship."

The strong emphasis on the outdoors and citizenship soon endeared Scouts and Scouting to both boys and adults across England. In 1909, American businessman William Boyce was visiting England and became lost in the famous London fog. A Boy Scout found him and, practicing the Scout Habit ("Do a good turn daily"), guided him to his destination. Impressed, Boyce was determined to bring the movement to America. In the spring of 1911, the Boy Scouts of America developed their own oath along the model of their British brethren.

Virtually nothing in America is the way it was in 1911—yet through decades that brought boom and bust, recession and depression, wars and rumors of war, changes in transportation, communication, and life-styles, the Scout Oath and the Scout Law have remained unchanged. They are intact for the same reason the Bill of Rights remains intact—they work. Yet our friend had spoken disparagingly of the virtues of being a "Boy Scout." Why? Had he too been "lost in the fog," thinking he should be applauded for acting unfairly to save the company money?

5:20 P.M. I absently creased my napkin into neat accordionlike folds while memories of my Scouting days flooded my mind. "It was a simpler world back when we were Boy Scouts," I said.

"Sure it was," my colleague replied. "We were pledged to keep the Scout Oath and obey the Scout Law. Sure, it was idealistic, but what's wrong with that? It's better to try to reach those kinds of goals *and fail* than not even try at all. Life would be simpler and better if everyone behaved like a *real Boy Scout.*"

"Yes, it would," I replied. "It would work in business just like it works for youth. It's the epitome of 'honesty is the best policy,' 'The customer is always right,' 'going the extra mile,' 'lending a helping hand,' and all of that. It's the Golden Rule expounded and explained."

My companion sipped his coffee and thoughtfully replaced the cup in the saucer. "I read an article in *Fortune* magazine some time back that said young workaholics are finding that family and volunteerism are becoming important again," he said. "They're learning you have to sow as well as reap to live a successful life or operate a successful business.

"The book of Proverbs says, 'As a man thinks, so he is.' If we keep thinking about the Boy Scout Oath and begin to *believe* it, pretty soon we'll *behave* it as well. Imagine the impact of a nation of *Business Scouts!* Imagine business people and employees who pledged to be trustworthy, loyal, helpful, friendly, courteous, kind, obedient, cheerful, thrifty, brave, clean, and reverent! Many businesses already operate by these values. If we all did, we just might regain our competitive advantage and be able to work together more collaboratively and successfully."

"Would people do it?" I asked.

"They used to. People helped one another build homes and raise barns. There was a time when an honest man could borrow money at the bank on a handshake. The beauty of the Scout Oath and Law is that they're like gravity—they work whether you believe in them or not. Whether you *want it to be that way or not!* A Scout is trustworthy, right? That's just another word for honesty. We grew up hearing 'honesty is the best policy.' Why? Because it's the best policy and the only policy that works. Oh, you can be dishonest and get away with it for a while—but in the end you may get what Ivan Boesky, the Watergate conspirators, Jim Bakker, and Leona Helmsley got. In the end, crime and sharp business practices don't pay. To paraphrase an adage, 'Time wounds all heels!' "

"What would happen if the Scout Oath were applied to American business?" I wondered, my mind whirling with possibilities. "It would change the way we do business from the *inside out*—not just the *outside in*! I think a lot of the best-selling business books have missed the need for internal change."

"Applying an external solution to an internal problem is like taking morphine for cancer. It may disguise the symptoms, but it doesn't do anything about the disease."

I nodded. "In fact, easing the pain can make it worse—because it can lull you into a false sense of security, a feeling that all is well when, in fact, all is wrong. It seems to me, a lot of people are trying to be successful while being *un*trustworthy, *dis*loyal, *un*helpful, *un*friendly, *dis*courteous, *un*kind, *dis*obedient, *un*cheerful, *un*thrifty, *un*brave, *un*clean, and *irreverent,*" I said.

My associate thought a moment before observing that many people operate on those premises. Executives and evangelists have been punished for playing fast and loose with the money of others. Stockbrokers were found guilty of insider trading. Executives at Beechnut, a large baby food company, were found guilty of selling phony apple juice. Several companies were indicted for selling adulterated orange juice, and one major supermarket chain, apparently sold it in full knowledge it wasn't pure, *because they got such a good buy*.

In February 1990, Bolar Pharmaceutical Company

was forced by the FDA to remove the largest-selling generic drug in America, a blood pressure medication taken by five hundred thousand people, because it was discovered the company switched test samples to get the drug approved. Earlier, in October 1989, Bolar had been forced to pull a generic antibiotic amid similar charges. These two drugs were taken by hundreds of thousands of people and accounted for 47 percent of the company's total sales. Executives had apparently decided to play fast and loose with the health of their customers.

When Watergate conspirator Jeb Stuart Magruder was asked how he had sunk to such a despicable level, he hung his head and said, "I don't know. I guess I just lost my moral compass." Is the real or perceived loss of moral compass the reason for the high level of distrust between management and labor? Could that be the explanation for the erosion of confidence in American products and preachers and politicians?

Whatever the cause, our work in the field of organizational change and leadership had convinced my associate and I that both management and employees feel a sense of frustration in their relationships. Lack of trust is common. Commitment to companies or customers has become an *uncommon* commodity. Little wonder America has lost the economic dominance it once enjoyed!

Today, when organizations strive to improve every aspect of their business, "total quality" has become the "in thing." Total quality is viewed as something innovative, earth shaking, and revolutionary. One only has to review the Scout Oath to understand how new it *isn't*.

"Somebody ought to write a book about it," I said to my colleague. "It would demonstrate how traditional values provide an organization's foundation, and that the foundation could stand the test of time."

* * *

6:10 P.M. They announced our flight, we paid our check, then boarded the plane, thinking about how the principles embodied in the Scout Oath and Law could work to the advantage of business everywhere.

The story you have just read is true, masked only slightly to disguise the identity of the client. The more we thought about those of *questionable* honor referring to those of *unquestioned* honor as "real Boy Scouts," the more convinced we became that believing and behaving the Boy Scout Oath and Law could favorably affect America and American business.

That's *our opinion.* You decide for yourself. If after you've read this book you conclude the authors are "Boy Scouts"—we consider that a true compliment.

CHAPTER TWO

ON MY HONOR, I WILL

—first line of Scout Oath

Sixty years ago, Costin J. Harrell wrote a devotional book that was destined to become a classic.[3] In this book, he related a story told him by Dr. W. F. Tillet of Vanderbilt University about ermine hunting in Europe. Dr. Tillet said the ermine honors his beautiful white coat to such an extent that it leads to his capture. When hunters find an ermine den, they daub the entrance with filth and loose the dogs. When the dogs get hot on the trail, the ermine runs for his den. However, when he arrives and finds he must soil his coat to enter, he turns to face the dogs and fight for his life. The ermine can be captured because he would rather have his coat

[3]*Walking with God*, Abingdon Press, 1928.

stained with blood than have it dirtied with filth. Honor is dearer than life!

Death Before Dishonor

In our youth, we watched swashbuckling movies. When honorable opponents were dueling with swords and one obtained the upper hand, he would ask his defeated foe, "Death or dishonor?" Everyone but the villain always chose death. Even in the land of make-believe, honor was dearer than life.

Few today would hold honor dearer than life. Many would not hold honor dearer than financial gain. Others would even sacrifice honor on the altar of expedience.

Perhaps our ambiguity toward honor is rooted in ignorance. Just what is *honor*? *Honor* is one of those words we all think we understand—until we're asked to provide the definition. We asked twenty executives to define the work and only *twelve* came reasonably close to the dictionary definition. What about you? Do you know what *honor* means? Think about it a moment before you read on.

If you had difficulty describing *honor*, you've got plenty of company! The point we're trying to make is that it is difficult to live up to an ill-defined standard. The dictionary also takes a couple of trips around the mulberry bush to define honor.

> **honor 1 a:** good name or public esteem: **REPUTATION b:** showing of usu. merited respect: **RECOGNITION 2: PRIVILEGE 3:** a person of superior standing—now used as a title for a holder of high office **4:** one whose worth brings respect or fame...**7: CHASTITY, PURITY 8 a:** a

keen sense of ethical conduct: INTEGRITY **b:** one's word given as a guarantee of performance.[4]

The definitions continue, but it is interesting that the kind of honor we are discussing doesn't appear until we get to the *eighth definition!* Since we find honor mentioned so often in the writings of our national patriarchs, we went back to the first American Dictionary[5], published by Noah Webster in 1828, to see how he defined it:

> True nobleness of mind; magnanimity; dignified respect for character, springing from probity, principle or moral rectitude; a distinguishing trait in the character of good men.

> An assumed appearance of nobleness; scorn of meanness, springing from the fear of reproach, without regard to principle.[5]

Notice how Noah Webster defined genuine honor succinctly and clearly—then immediately warned against counterfeits! It's true that not everyone who speaks of honor has it. Ralph Waldo Emerson wrote of one guest, "The louder he talked of his honor, the faster we counted our spoons."

We've all heard the expression "There's even honor among thieves." Is there? In 1973, Bobby Joe Reickenbacker, the infamous "Bandanna Bandit," was sentenced to 320 years in prison for a series of daring bank robberies. Now reformed and released, Bobby

[4]*Webster's New Collegiate Dictionary,* Merriam-Webster, Inc., 1975.
[5]Noah Webster, *An American Dictionary of the English Language,* 1828.

Joe counsels teenagers. He says, "My father was a thief, and from the time I was eleven years old, I wanted to be a big-time bandit like he was. I've been a thief and I've been surrounded by thousands of thieves most of my life. My stealing got me into reform school, city jail, county jail, and state and federal prison. I can say without a moment's hesitation that there is no honor among thieves. That's an illusion fostered by social workers and writers. How can there possibly be honor among the dishonorable? We thieves stole from each other in prison, just like we did when we were on the outside."

Bobby Joe is right. If there were "honor among thieves," they wouldn't be thieves. A person either has honor or he doesn't. Honor isn't honor if you can turn it on and off. There can be no mixture of light and darkness, of honor and dishonor.

It's impossible to hold two diametrically opposing value systems in our mind for any length of time. When we try to mix honor and dishonor, we create stresses that shatter our consciences, careers, and companies. The result is that the "honor" we tout is not genuine, but false honor, the loud, brassy, hollow kind that causes others to question our motives and count their spoons.

The fact that false honor exists should not make us skeptical about honor. The false never diminishes the value of the original as long as we can distinguish between the two. If anything, fakes only make the original even more valuable and beautiful. When a Scout proclaims, "On my honor, I will," he isn't talking about assumed or artificial honor, he's talking about the genuine article. He is saying *he will*, based on his "nobleness of mind, magnanimity, dignified respect for character."

"Scout's honor" is the kind of honor Jefferson wrote

about in the Declaration of Independence: "We mutually pledge to each other our lives, our fortunes, our sacred honor."

It is what Congress had in mind when it created the Medal of Honor. The medal was conceived to honor a soldier whose own personal sense of honor caused him to "distinguish himself conspicuously by gallantry and intrepidity at the risk of his life, above and beyond the call of duty." It is fitting that the nation's highest award goes to those who hold honor dearer than life.

We've been working on the definition of *honor*. What is an "honorable person" or an "honorable organization"? We believe the easiest definition is that an honorable person or organization is one that does the "right thing" regardless of whether or not it's the convenient thing, the profitable thing, or the fun thing. Honor is doing what's right, regardless of the consequences. Honor is making commitments and keeping them.

Many American businesses and business people *do believe* that honor is sacred. Throughout this book you'll find examples of leaders and organizations who have made the commitment to honor and integrity. Not surprisingly, these individuals and organizations are typically recognized leaders in their fields. These are not supersaints or moral monks—they are ordinary people with an extraordinary commitment to honor and integrity. We each have the ability to do the same. All we need to succeed is commitment and hard work.

NOT EVERYONE IN A DISHONORABLE SITUATION IS DISHONORABLE

There are some who rationalize their behavior for the sake of expediency or gain. Like the ermine, honor and integrity may cost us our survival. Whatever the cost, persons of honor behave honorably. Because of this, it is possible to retain your honor even in a situation that many consider "dishonorable."

For instance, many passengers felt Braniff International Airways did not act honorably during their first bankruptcy. Many people were irate when Braniff recalled planes in flight, stranding passengers and not refunding the price of tickets. While the corporate honor was sullied, most of those who came under attack—travel agents, flight attendants, pilots, and even President Howard Putnam—were innocent victims themselves.

When the board of directors at Braniff first contacted Putnam about becoming president of Braniff, he was president of Southwest Airlines, a regional carrier. Putnam took the job and promised the board to do his best. As soon as he took office, he realized the airline only had a ten-day cash reserve. If he stayed in his post, there was only a slight chance he could save the airline. If he left immediately, he could probably get another job and avoid a black mark on his record. Yet he had made a promise on his honor—and felt a promise made was a debt unpaid. He decided to stay with Braniff, do what he could to save it, and if he couldn't, ride the plane down along with everyone else.

In retrospect, it was Putnam's honor that contributed to the airline's demise. In the waning days of Braniff's fight to continue operating, a reporter asked Putnam if he could guarantee that Braniff would be flying in a year. Putnam, in a sense putting professional death before dishonor, stated he couldn't—resulting in further negative publicity. Yet, in the end, honor won out. Not one shareholder filed suit against Braniff or Braniff Management during the bankruptcy proceedings.

Harvard University now conducts a course entitled Ethics of a Bankruptcy, based on Putnam's handling of this difficult situation. Putnam has gone on to a successful career as an entrepreneur and currently shares his leadership experience with many of the country's best-managed organizations.

Another case is William Reynolds, heir to the R. J. Reynolds tobacco founders. His own sense of honor refused to take refuge in the smoke screen covering the health issue surrounding tobacco use. He not only disposed of his R. J. Reynolds stock, he is an antitobacco crusader and volunteers to do antismoking ads for the American Cancer Society. Reynolds gave up personal opportunity for honor. One might even say he gave up his birthright for his sacred honor.

BE TRUE TO YOURSELF

The January 16, 1990, issue of *Parents' Magazine* reported that 78 percent of respondents in a poll expressed a desire to return to "traditional values and old-fashioned morality." This is something we must do if we are to survive, as a society.

If we are to be people of honor, we must begin by being honest about our intents and motives. If we want to become a person of honor, we must begin by being honest about our motivation. Once we accept personal responsibility for our behavior and start being totally honest with ourselves, we'll find we "cannot be false to any man."

Honor is a learned behavior. Our children, our co-workers, our employees, learn honor from us. They learn more by *observation* than they do by *conversation*.

Sometimes, they can't hear what we're *saying* because what we're *doing* speaks so loudly.

Little people steal little things because they see big people steal big things with impunity. Little people tell little lies because they hear big shots tell big ones. Why shouldn't an employee falsify a test report on a single component when he sees his supervisor sign off on a big one that's defective? Why shouldn't a secretary take office supplies home when she sees her employer overcharge a customer?

We tell our children, "It's not whether you win or lose, but how you play the game." What they often see by our actions, however, is: "It's not whether you win or lose, it's whether you win!"

PEOPLE OF HONOR—PEOPLE OF ACTION

The power of the Scout Oath as a business guide is grounded in honor. But the "juice flows" when we add the words *I will*. Like the positive pole of an electrical charge, the two simple words *I will* provide the behavioral example of honor.

Unfortunately, there are many who have adopted the approach of "On my honor, I will think about it," or "On my honor, I'll let others take responsibility for that decision." The Scout Oath is an active affirmation. Honor is the qualifier, but action is the order of the day. Scouts try to do a good turn daily. Somehow, the picture wouldn't be right if the Scout on the corner simply pointed the elderly lady in the right direction, then nudged her into the intersection. It is by positive action that we demonstrate honor, and by honor that we distinguish ourselves from those who do not uphold these high ideals.

People of honor don't look for escape clauses or excuses or justifications. They're more concerned with *what's right* than with *who's right*. There isn't one standard of conduct for presidents and governors and another for businessmen and shopkeepers. There's one set of standards for everyone, and we are each judged by how we measure against them.

We assume no one reading this book has lived a totally honorable life—certainly neither of us writing it has. However, one robin does not make a spring, and one dishonorable deed does not make a dishonorable person. Many dishonorable acts are committed by decent, honorable human beings who, unfortunately, lost sight of what is right amidst a momentary lapse into desperation or weakness. Circumstances convince them that bending the rules is acceptable "just this once." After the first lapse, it becomes easier, and so a habit of deceit and deception is developed.

We are what we habitually do. If we are habitually unreliable, undependable, and dishonorable, we become that. On the other hand, if we make commitments and keep them, if our word is our bond, *regardless of the cost,* then we become what we have been behaving. We become a person of integrity by behaving like a person of integrity.

Honorable people not only do honorable things, they do them with honorable motives. The more honorable we are, the more we positively affect those around us.

A man went into a grocery store and stood in a long line to hand the checker a quarter. When she asked, "What's that for?" he said, "The Coke machine gave me too much change." A teenager in line behind him gawked, then silently took the candy bar out of his pocket and put it on the counter with his other purchases.

When Mark White became governor of Texas, he was concerned that high school students who were failing academically were playing team sports. He felt they could better devote the time to their schoolwork than to team practice and pushed a "no pass/no play" rule through the legislature. He did this in full knowledge that Texans love football as much as anyone else, and it could well spell political suicide for him—yet he did it anyway, because he felt it was the right thing to do. When Congresswoman Jeannette Rankin voted against the United States entering World War II the day after the Japanese bombed Pearl Harbor, her political career ended. Not many Americans agreed with her point of view, but no one doubted her integrity or that she felt honor bound to do what she thought was right, regardless of the consequences.

CORPORATIONS OF HONOR

History is replete with examples of corporate honor and commitment. There aren't enough pages in this book to make an exhaustive list of companies, much less the deeds themselves. However, here are a few that come immediately to mind. You will hear about others throughout this book.

Reader's Digest was the first magazine to drop cigarette advertising, back when the first surgeon general's warning about smoking and cancer was released. This cost the magazine millions in lost revenues. They did it because they felt committed to providing their readers long life and health as well as reading enjoyment.

A. E. Staley Corporation makes corn syrup for major soft drink companies. Their concept of corporate honor says that workers are important and have valuable skills and ideas. So in 1977, they began creating "self-managing" teams to help improve the way they work together. They honor their commitment to this idea by allowing teams to spend as much time as they need training, teaching, and helping one another.

I.B.M. has a history of respect for the individual, customer service, and excellence that goes back to the 1930s. They have responded to tough times in the computer industry by managing their restructuring through transfers, early retirement and a liberal voluntary severance package that operationalizes their beliefs. I.B.M. has been ahead of its time in other ways too. They started job enrichment in the 1920s and a version of "quality circles" in the 1930s.

Soft Sheen Products, Inc., founded by Edward and Bethann Gardner, is the largest minority-owned manufacturing firm in the country, with sales over $87 million in 1989. But the business goes beyond profits for the Gardner family. Soft Sheen makes a concerted effort to provide jobs for the black community and an opportunity to enhance black self-esteem through quality products.

Hallmark Cards, Inc., is the world's largest greeting card company and widely considered one of the best places in America to work. (Hallmark was listed in *The 100 Best Companies to Work for in America,* by Robert Levering, Milton Moskowitz and Michael Katz, Addison-Wesley, 1984.) Hallmark is one of the few businesses that has a tradition of full employment without layoffs. In addition, they offer some of the best employee benefits of any company. Most notably, Hallmark's sense of corporate commitment to employees includes interest-free loans for emergencies, college loans for education, physical fitness facilities, and covered parking for those working at the Crown Center complex (a great benefit during harsh winters). Their commitment to quality gives production employees the right to stop the presses if they feel the product does not meet Hallmark's standards.

Carnegie Steel (U.S. Steel) was founded by Andrew Carnegie, an immigrant whose first job was as a bobbin boy in a cotton factory for twenty cents a day. He built Carnegie Steel Company into one of the largest corporations in America, and when he retired, in 1901, had a fortune of half a billion dollars. He felt it was a sin to die rich and wrote in his *Gospel of Wealth* that rich men are trustees of their wealth with a fiduciary responsibility to use it for public good. Consequently, he committed more than $350 million in his lifetime, building schools, universities, and libraries all across America.

In addition to sharing his wealth with the public, he shared it with those on his payroll. With the exception of the Homestead strike,[6] which occurred while he was out of the country, his labor relations were always good. He often said, "Capital, labor and employer [are] a three-legged stool, none before or after the others, all equally indispensable." He once wrote, "I believe that higher wages to men who respect their employers and are happy and contented are a good investment, yielding, indeed, big dividends."[7] Over twenty-nine of his executives became millionaires in their own rights.

Carnegie was shrewd and sharp, but fair, honest, and compassionate. He enjoyed making money and enjoyed

[6]Improvements in manufacturing processes had increased production at the mill by 60 percent and Carnegie had 218 workers who were under contract to be paid so much per ton of steel produced. When the contract was up, the company asked that they split the difference and the workers take a 30 percent wage hike as the 60 percent increase in tonnage was because of the new process, not the workers themselves. The union refused the offer and a bitter strike followed.

[7]*The Autobiography of Andrew Carnegie*, Houghton Mifflin Company, 1920.

sharing its benefits with others. At a time when industrialists were universally characterized as "robber barons," honor was dearer to him than making a quick dollar. He demonstrated it through action and reaped the rewards of success.

The Freeman Companies grew from a party decorating company in 1923 to become one of the largest staging and decorating corporations in the United States. In 1981, President Don Freeman announced an employee stock ownership plan for the company to transfer ownership from the family to the employees. Today, most ESOPs are done by public companies to avert a hostile takeover. However, Freeman was a family-owned company, and the sole reason was to reward the employees who had made the company grow and prosper.

How well is the program working? Sales in 1981 were $45 million and by 1989 had soared to $190 million—up 422 percent! By the end of fiscal year 1989, 23 percent of corporate stock had been placed in employee hands. The ESOP had worked so well, the family voted to transfer an *additional 23 percent in the decade of the nineties!* Freeman didn't just *talk about making a commitment*—he honored it.

ARE YOU A PERSON OF HONOR?

Would you like a quick and easy way of determining your own sense of honor or that of your co-workers or employees? Simply answer this question: *Who are your five favorite heroes or heroines?* You can tell a lot about yourself or others by the answers you get!

Before you read further, stop now and list your five favorite heroes or heroines. They can be from the pages of history, of faith, or of fiction—don't stop and think about it, just do it right off the top of your head!

My Five Favorite Heroes or Heroines

(order unimportant)

1. _____
2. _____
3. _____
4. _____
5. _____

Look at your list. What does it reveal about yourself and your sense of honor and integrity? Do you try to emulate those you admire? Most people do!

The problem with honor, as we said at the onset, is that some people have no clear idea of its definition. When Harvard Business School began teaching ethics as well as business principles, John McArthur, dean of the school, started encouraging students not to "go through life focused only on number one." According to a *Wall Street Journal* article, Albert Gordon, a Harvard fund-raiser and chairman emeritus of Kidder Peabody, said, "I hope they don't take the ethics issue too far ... they run the risk that some students could decide to go to other schools in the future."

Dean McArthur added an ethics question to the admission test. It asks students to explain how they have managed an ethical dilemma they have experienced. Laura Gordon Fisher, the school's admissions director says, "It's amazing how many people admit they've never experienced a moral dilemma. Some applicants want to know if they should fabricate one."

Either those students live in a "kinder, gentler world" than the rest of us or they lack a moral compass to tell them when they face a dilemma.

The Bottom Line

People today want action anchored by integrity in their leaders, associates, and friends. Everyone wishes *everyone else* were that way, but it must begin with each of us. If our nation and our organizations are to continue to thrive or even survive in the nineties and beyond, we must become people of honor, integrity, and commitment. These ideas may sound simplistic, but profound truths often appear simplistic to skeptics.

People have a right to be skeptical about integrity. They've been lied to and misled before. How do you convince others that you're serious about your commitment? Try saying, "On my honor, I will"—*then do it!* That, of course, is the key: *doing it.* An adage says, "The road to hell is paved with good intentions." *Thinking* a good game is not the same as *playing a good game.* Thinking a good deed is not the same as doing a good deed. Inaction cannot be compensated for by thinking, Wasn't it nice of me to have *thought* about doing that!

Once you put hands and feet on your commitment and follow through, you'll become known as a person of honor—because you'll be a person of honor! You won't have to talk about your honor, other people will talk about it instead. As D. L. Moody said, "We are told to let our light shine, and if it does, we won't need to tell anybody it does. Lighthouses don't fire cannons to call attention to their shining—they just shine."

Six Steps to Becoming a Person of Honor

1. Establish the habit of focusing on what's right rather than who's right.
2. Develop a list of honorable heroes and heroines. Learn everything you can about them. Make these people your personal "board of directors," and when you're faced with a moral dilemma, ask yourself what they would do.
3. Consciously associate with people of integrity. Seek out co-workers, neighbors, mentors, and employers who demonstrate their integrity and commitment. They'll be easy to spot once you know what to look for. They'll have a reputation for integrity, responsibility, and helping others.
4. Regularly spend time in self-evaluation. Evaluate your actions against the actions of other honorable and committed individuals when you're faced with a tough decision.
5. Accept complete responsibility for your actions, especially when it's convenient to blame others. Actively accepting responsibility forces us to evaluate the impact of our decisions prior to our actions.
6. Stand by your beliefs, even when they appear unpopular. Compromise on implementation and interpretation, never on principles. Whenever possible, work for solutions that meet everyone's needs, but never sacrifice the integrity and honesty of your beliefs on the altar of convenience.

"ON MY HONOR, I WILL"

You will find a fill-in-the-blank section at the end of each remaining chapter. Its purpose is to allow you the opportunity to make your own commitments. We hope you'll use the time and space to reflect on things you're currently doing that are consistent with the material covered in each chapter. Most important, we hope you'll set specific goals for yourself in areas where you want to grow or improve.

In the space below, list some commitments you wish to make regarding your personal honor and actions.

On my honor, I will:

- _____
  _____
  _____

- _____
  _____
  _____

- _____
  _____
  _____

- _____
  _____
  _____

- _____
  _____
  _____

- _____
  _____
  _____

- _____

_____

_____

• _____

_____

_____

CHAPTER THREE

On my honor, I will

DO MY BEST

Lives of great men all remind us
We too can make our lives sublime
And departing, leave behind us
Footprints on the sands of time.

—LONGFELLOW

While we appreciate Longfellow's sentiments, few of us will leave footprints on the sands of time that more than a handful would ever notice. Columbus, explorer of the New World, left footprints that opened the way for exploration and colonization. Schweitzer, missionary doctor to Africa, left footprints in unexplored jungles. Chuck Yeager, the first man to fly faster than the speed of sound, left footprints in the sky. Neil Armstrong, first man on the moon, left footprints on the lunar sands. Albert Einstein, developer of the theory of relativity, left footprints into the universe.

We could go on and on, naming names like Louis Pasteur, Jonas Salk, Florence Nightingale, Booker T. Washington, George Washington Carver, and Martin

Luther King, Jr. Who wouldn't like to be a genuine American hero, even if it were only for the fifteen minutes Andy Warhol promised? We may have neither the ability nor the opportunity to be a hero to millions, but each of us has the opportunity to do our best every day. And, by doing so, leave our own, albeit humble, footsteps on the sands of time.

We may never be counted among the world's best, but we should always be counted on to do our best. Each of us is being watched by others, to see how we handle temptations and challenges. When those around us see us doing our best day in and day out, we inspire them to do the same. If we inspire others by example, then in our own way, we are leaving footprints on the sands of time. True greatness requires motive, means, and opportunity.

We often associate greatness with fame. We glamorize others' actions and assign them hero status. There's nothing wrong with heroes. We need more of them as role models in our world. But, we must not think less of ourselves because we have not or cannot achieve hero status. The fame we associate with heroism requires more than greatness—it often requires special circumstances. Could Audie Murphy have been the most decorated American soldier if he had been drafted in peacetime? What if Mary Lou Retton had been born before the modern Olympics? What if George Washington Carver had been born in an area that hadn't grown sweet potatoes and peanuts? Could Roger Staubach have been a hero if he'd been born in a place or time when football wasn't the king of sports? Of course not. So while *part* of being a hero—of being the best— comes from within, some of it comes from without. For this reason, you can't judge yourself harshly just because situations do not come along to prove your heroic qualities.

Most of the people we call heroes were going about their business, doing what they do best when the special circumstances arrived. An old motivational speaker liked to say, "When opportunity knocks, you have to jump up and answer the door!" "How do you know it's opportunity?" someone in the audience would invariably ask. He would answer, "You don't. You have to keep jumping!"

Roger Staubach writes in *Winning Strategies in Selling* about the role events outside our control play in success. A quarterback has no control over the field position his team has when he gets the ball. He said if the defensive team gives you the ball in good field position, then you're in a good position to be a hero. On the other hand, if you get the ball deep in your own territory, being a hero isn't as easy.

In life, some of us inherit better field positions than others. If your ancestors' heights ran from five six to five eight, you're in poor field position to be a professional basketball star. There *have been* short basketball stars—Spud Webb of the Atlanta Hawks is an excellent example. Though less that five eight, he is a true superstar and has won the NBA dunking contest against players a foot and a half taller! Basketball today is a game of giants, well above average height. A player of *less than average height,* like Spud, has his work cut out to be a hero. Spud couldn't do a thing about his "field position," all he could do was do his best—and that was enough to make him a superstar.

That's the point. A good field position is a blessing, but poor field positions can be overcome. For example, if you have musical interests and are born into a musical family, you are in an excellent field position. If you have musical interests and are born into a family that can't afford lessons, you have a poorer field position, but you can still score—as evidenced by the success of singer Ray Charles.

We each have the ability to be "the best *we can be*" and, in doing our best, we become great even if we don't become famous. Should a surgeon give up his practice just because he or she isn't the world's leading surgeon? Should an actor forsake the theater because he isn't as famous as Laurence Olivier? Must a pilot turn in his wings because he'll never be a "top gun"? Should a mother place her children in an orphanage because she'll never be "mother of the year"? Should a salesperson resign because he or she will never be the top salesperson in the company? Should a teacher abandon her class because she has no geniuses to inspire? Of course not! We work within whatever field position we have. We overcome obstacles or we go around them. We give each situation, each challenge, and each opportunity our best shot.

We become great by using our motives, means, and opportunities to work continually toward being our best. If special circumstances present themselves, we may achieve fame, but that's icing on the cake. The true superstar was great before he or she became famous, and many famous people are not great at anything.

A golfing buddy once lost a round by twelve strokes and was ecstatic! Even though he had "lost" the game, he had played the best game of golf in his life. He was happy because he wasn't trying to beat *his opponent's score*—he was trying to beat *his own best score*.

Being *the best* was not as important to him as doing *his best*. The same is true with each of us. You may never be the best that *can be*—but you can be the best *you* can *be*. You can be better tomorrow than you are today and better next week than you are tomorrow. It takes time and it takes training and it takes dedication—but you can do it. You can succeed because you're not in a game where there's only one winner and everyone else is a loser. You're in the game of life, a game in which everyone can be a winner. You're not competing against the best in the world, you're competing against your own previous best effort. The only record you're trying to beat is your own.

Film star Ingrid Bergman, in her autobiography, *My Story*, relates that she was always driven to do her best in every scene. Many times, she insisted on redoing a scene that everyone else thought was fine the way it was. Finally, she'd say, "Well, that was good—but I'll do better later." She said it so often on one film that the crew began good-naturedly calling her "Betterlater"!

A close friend of ours has children who are competitive swimmers. Before a meet, he tells them, "It isn't important whether or not you win a ribbon. It's not important that you *be the best*—what's important is that you *do your best*. If you do that, your mother and I will be proud of you and, more important, you'll be proud of yourselves and you'll have fun."

In our careers and in our relationships with others, we can be proud of ourselves when we do our best. If we do that, we may still fail to reach the goals we set for ourselves, but we'll "fail forward." That is, we will fail reaching toward the mark. We will come closer to the mark than we ever did before. And when we fail forward, chances are we will ultimately go the full distance.

Until the Korean War, Americans viewed themselves as the biggest and best at everything. We had entered the nineteenth century certain we had a "manifest destiny" to stretch our borders from sea to shining sea. We flexed our muscles in the Spanish-American War, then entered World War I confident we could "lick the Hun." We emerged from that war as a world leader. In World War II, we entered confident we could fight enemies on two sides of the globe and win. We emerged from that war as the dominant world power. While the rest of the world lay in shambles, America was strong and rich and free and confident.

Our optimism carried over into our business and commerce. The industrial revolution achieved its greatest moments in this country. The inventors and inventions that sparked the information age were "Made in the USA," and those words defined quality. During the fifties, "Made in Japan" meant junk to us. Then the Japanese decided they needed some American know-how to rebuild and compete. They hired an American, W. Edwards Deming, to teach them the true meaning of quality.

What happened next? Japanese businesses began concentrating on quality. Meanwhile, many American businesses began thinking that quick returns were more important than quality. Consequently, many American businesses began "doing what's required" instead of "doing what's best." Performance slipped, bringing down quality, dependability, and service. Workers in other parts of the world began producing to the American standard of quality at a lower cost. Our balance of payments shifted out of kilter as our fellow citizens began buying foreign goods that were of equal or greater quality and lower in cost.

We saw the result of our actions, but too often we failed to focus on "what's wrong?" and preferred instead to find "who's wrong?" Management blamed workers, lamenting, "Workers have changed! They don't

care about a day's work for a day's pay anymore."
Workers blamed management, claiming, "Management
is getting what they deserve. We want to do a good job,
but they're more interested in quantity than quality."

While we argue and point fingers, in the minds of
many "Made in Japan" has become synonymous with
high quality and value. Meanwhile, some have come to
consider "Made in the USA" synonymous with low
quality and poor value.

Today, we are sensing a resurgence of America's
traditional commitment to quality, service, and value. It
has again become fashionable to "do my best." Words
like *quality, excellence,* and *service* are again becoming the
maxims by which we manage and lead.

Tom Peters and Robert Waterman encouraged us to
"search for excellence," to thrive on chaos and renew
our organizations. W. Edwards Deming, the American
prophet of quality who first taught the Japanese how to
compete, has now found acceptance in his own land.
After him, Philip Crosby, Dr. J. M. Juran, and others
have imparted their own unique management wisdom,
while Ron Zemke, Karl Albrecht, and others have ex-
panded the concept of quality from the manufacturing
arena to other areas of service.

Today, American products are again being honored
for quality, and we have begun to regain some of the
markets we lost. However, we still have a long way to go
before American products regain their dominance in
the marketplaces of the world. The key to our success
in reclaiming our market share is not merely to focus
on being the best, but to emphasize doing our best
each day.

History gives us many examples of American leaders
who focused on doing their best to fill a need or meet a
challenge.

Edison, who failed thousands of times before perfecting the incandescent light bulb, taught us the value of innovation, research, and persistence. After years of futile attempts, Chester Carlson invented the first xerographic copier—teaching us the value of persistence and belief in a goal.

Had either of these men focused only on "being the best," they might never have achieved their goal. They might have given up and tried to take an easier road to the top. Instead, they "did their best" each day and eventually succeeded.

In 1930, Vannevar Bush built the first modern analog computer. Later, John Atanasoff, a professor at Iowa State, built a better one. Although Atanasoff's computer could only add and subtract up to eight digits, he laid the groundwork for others. In 1944, Howard Aiken built the first digital computer controlled by vacuum tubes. He called it an Electronic Numerical Integrator and Computer (ENIAC). ENIAC, in turn, laid the foundation for the modern PC.

Not every individual who focuses on doing his best revolutionizes business, but every individual who focuses on doing his best can and does make a contribution. Our "footprints on the sands of time" may not appear in history books, but they can influence the opportunities of others. Who's to say that a business leader doing his or her best won't provide the environment for a major technological breakthrough? Who's to say that a parent doing his or her best isn't shaping the life of a future U.S. president? At the very least, they are helping to shape their child's values and ideals.

As individuals and organizations, we have an opportunity to leave our footprints on the sands of time by doing our best each day. Einstein had a teacher. Lincoln had a role model. Carver had someone who instilled a desire to learn. Retton had a coach. Without these often unknown people doing their best, we might never have been influenced by those who became the best!

Why don't we each do our best? The sad truth is, many want to leave the difficult tasks to someone else, focusing on expedience at the expense of quality. A few others find it easier to let others do it all and reap the rewards. There have always been some shirkers, but it wasn't until the time of the Korean War that shirking became endemic in America.

During the Korean War, the army found that 100 percent of the fighting was done by 30 percent of the combat soldiers. This doesn't include the support and supply personnel—a staggering 70 percent of those soldiers who were in combat situations never fired their weapons. A study showed there were four primary reasons why most soldiers chose not to fight:

1. **They lacked confidence in their weapons**. The U.S. Army had the most sophisticated, reliable, advanced weapons in the world, but their soldiers lacked confidence in them! They were afraid they would get in a difficult situation and their weapons would fail to protect them.
2. **They liked to rely on heavy artillery and aerial bombardment.** In this war, America had air superiority. The troops in the field thought it was better to just wait and let the planes and the big guns do the fighting. It took less time, trouble, and risk to call for bombardment than it did to fight. Besides, the guns were heavy, cumbersome, and had heavy recoil. (We tried to negate this objection in Vietnam by going from a .30 to a .22 caliber in our main battle rifle and from .45 to 9 mm [.38 caliber] in sidearms.)

3. **They didn't like to expose themselves to enemy fire.** They felt the enemy would fire back at anyone who fired at them. If you stayed down and kept low, you might go unnoticed.
4. **They liked to take the line of least resistance.** Doing nothing is always easier than doing something. It was easier to hole up and wait than it was to move forward and perhaps fail.

This survey in no way depreciates the actions of the many heroic soldiers who displayed gallantry and bravery in the face of the enemy in Korea. It merely points out that many are content if their outfit "*is* the best." They do not feel a personal obligation to "*do* their best" in order to keep it that way.

Our purpose is not to evaluate our national performance on the battlefield but our performance on the competitive field of commerce. Yet there is something to be learned from our study of fighting men in Korea. Today, many workers and managers are not "doing their best" because of similar reasons.

1. **They lack confidence in their weapons.** They aren't certain their products and their processes are as good as their competitor's. They aren't certain of their corporate or personal commitment to "be the best."
2. **They like to rely on heavy artillery and aerial bombardment to accomplish their objectives.** How do we "bomb" our competition in business? With marketing muscle, advertising, and promotion. Many salespeople feel the solution doesn't lie in their own hard work but in better ads. Many production people feel the solution lies not in their producing a better product but in someone hiring better salespeople.

3. **They don't like to expose themselves to enemy fire.** If you move out aggressively, your enemies will notice you. Some hang back hoping to "hide in a crack where the competition can't find them." While it does make sense to pick your opportunities, once you're in the contest, you must face your competition head on in order to survive. Unfortunately, even successful companies often reward *not failing* more than they reward *initiative*. Therefore, their "troops" hesitate to stick their necks out, feeling, "If I don't risk anything, I won't lose anything."

4. **They like to take the line of least resistance.** It takes less effort to fail than it does to succeed. No one questions you if you do it the way you have always done it. If you try something new and it doesn't work, you have to explain, and then you might lapse into reason number 3.

We have often heard of the 80/20 rule. Applied to sales, it means that roughly 80 percent of the sales are made by 20 percent of the salespeople. Applied to productivity, many management gurus translate that rule to mean 80 percent of the work is accomplished by 20 percent of the workforce. The authors have collectively worked with well over three hundred organizations and corporations, and we do not accept those percentages. We feel the percentage of superior performers is much, much higher. However, we acknowledge there is plenty of room for improvement. If every individual focused on doing his or her best, we would begin to focus on "*how* should I?" instead of "*why* should I?" When we ask "how?" questions, we tend to find the right answers!

COMPETITION MAKES US BETTER

How do we instill this desire to "do our best" in ourselves and others? One way is through competition. Healthy competition challenges us to new heights and helps build the desire to do our best. What do you do if you're head and shoulders above the competition? Well, then you play against your own best efforts.

A sixteenth-century samurai named Miyamoto Musashi had the problem of being so much better than his competition that he found himself bored. He had become a swordsman of legendary proportions and once defeated 150 samurai in a single battle. Like gunfighters in the American West, as his reputation grew, so did the number of people willing to challenge him. Scarcely a week went by that some up-and-coming swordslinger didn't challenge him to a duel. Musashi grew tired of killing, yet he could not refuse a challenge without losing face. Finally, he compromised by carving himself a wooden sword and fighting with that!

By using a wooden sword, he was able to rise to the challenge, keep his competitive spirit, save face, and also save the lives of his adversaries. He never stopped proving he was the best swordsman in Japan—and lived to die of natural causes.

Healthy competition is a great tool for pushing ourselves and others toward doing their best, but certain kinds of competition can be unhealthy. "Winning is everything" has, unfortunately, often been interpreted as winning at all costs. That kind of competition is neither healthy nor friendly. It builds adversaries rather than respected competitors and is a major force behind the cynicism and lack of trust that exist in many businesses. If we do "whatever it takes" to win in one area, what's to keep us from doing the same in another?

Healthy competition comes when we approach life and work with a desire to "do my best every day." That focuses the competition internally instead of just externally. That encourages us to compete with ourselves, not with others. That enables us to be team players—because if we're competing against ourselves, then each person on the team can emerge a winner—even if the team should lose.

What does it take to do your best today and every day? It takes five things: **purpose, responsibility, commitment, flexibility,** and **support.** Let's examine each separately.

1. Purpose (You must have a reason to do your best.) When Alice met the Cheshire Cat in *Alice in Wonderland,* she asked, "Would you tell me, please, which way I ought to go from here?"

"That depends a good deal on where you want to get to," said the Cat.

"I don't much care where—" said Alice.

"Then it doesn't matter which way you go," said the Cat.

The Cat's point was well taken. If we don't know where we're going, then one path is as good as another. It is only when we have a purpose and a destination that the road we take becomes important.

Dennis McCuistion, consultant, author,[8] and talk show host, often asks people to define and write down their mission in addition to their goals. An individual's mission, like an organization's, provides the overriding purpose against which goals can be evaluated. Doing your best for the sake of doing your best is difficult to maintain over long periods. Purpose provides direction and internal motivation.

[8]*The Prevention and Collection of Problem Loans*, Bank Administration Institute, 1989. *Selling Strategies for Today's Bankers: A Survival Guide for Tomorrow,* Dearborn Press, 1990.

2. Commitment (You must tenaciously work toward your goal.) Commitment is what occurs when desire and self-discipline come together. It's an inward desire to achieve your best because you want to, not because you have to. It is commitment that keeps you going in spite of discouragement, disillusionment, and defeat. It is commitment that keeps you practicing, preparing, and producing when it would be easier to call it quits.

Calvin Coolidge, thirtieth President of the United States, had this to say about the importance of commitment.

> Press on: Nothing in the world can take the place of persistence. Talent will not; nothing is more common than unsuccessful individuals with talent. Genius will not; unrewarded genius is almost a proverb. Education will not; the world is full of educated derelicts. Persistence and determination alone are omnipotent.

Occasional brilliance does not consistently win races. Consistent effort is the mark of true commitment. An admirer once told Van Cliburn, "I'd give my life to be able to play the piano like that!" Van Cliburn replied, "I did."

Desire comes from within, but the self-discipline required to demonstrate your commitment must be learned. Consider establishing a daily plan to help you develop successful habits. The plan should include specific goals, both immediate and long-range, that move you forward. It should also include the activities you need to perform every day to meet your goals. The first few days will be difficult. Remember how you felt on the second day of your new exercise program? But after a month or so, you'll find yourself with new habits that propel you toward your desired purpose. Many people desire to be their best. It is the only those who combine desire with self-discipline who have the commitment to really *be* their best.

3. Responsibility (You must hold yourself accountable for your choices.) Successful individuals understand cause and effect relationships: we reap what we sow. In computer jargon, the catchphrase is GI/GO. Usually, GI/GO means "garbage in/garbage out," but it can also mean "good in/good out." The interesting thing about sowing and reaping is that the harvest is inevitably larger than the planting. If we plant beans in our garden, we get beans back—multiplied. If we were foolish enough to plant thistles in our garden, we would reap thistles—multiplied.

When we take personal responsibility for our successes and failures, we begin looking for "ways" instead of "outs." We lose the ability to learn from our mistakes when we try to rationalize failures. Begin replacing excuses such as "they told me to" and "it's not my fault because" with winning phrases such as "I made a mistake but I have learned" and "it was my responsibility."

4. Flexibility (You must be willing to creatively adapt to change.) There are seven words that shackle organizations and people to the past. They are: "We've never done it this way before!" Benjamin Franklin said, "Don't look for the birds of this year in the nests of the last." Today, change doesn't just come annually, but monthly, weekly, and even daily. Tradition has its place, but hidebound tradition can cause us to lose our competitive edge as organizations and individuals. One client described his organization as thirty-three years of tradition unmarred by progress! We have to be flexible enough to break with tradition if we're going to turn obstacles into opportunities.

Beethoven began to lose his hearing in his twenties, yet he had learned the sound of music so well that he could compose in his mind. Some of his greatest masterpieces were created after the composer was unable to hear a single note of music! Milton, the poet, went blind—yet he taught himself to compose in his head and dictated to his daughters. O. J. Simpson and Wilma Rudolph both wore leg braces as children, yet they overcame their handicaps to become great athletes. As Renoir's arthritis became so bad he couldn't hold a paint brush, he had friends tie a brush to his hand—and continued painting. Moreover, he *continued painting masterpieces!*

When you face adversity, be flexible and open to alternate routes. As Zig Ziglar says, "When life hands you a lemon, make lemonade."

5. Support (You must have others on your team.) A good quarterback can help make a football team great, but a team is more than a quarterback. No matter how good a player is, he can't play all the positions. When time is running out, it's good to know that there are others to call on for support who share your commitment and your mission. The quarterback may get most of the attention, but he is quick to remind everyone of his support team, because without it, he'd never be able to move the ball.

The value of support is shown by successful programs such as Weight Watchers and Alcoholics Anonymous. In AA, each member is assigned a support person because *they* realize that the fight to do their best every day is often overwhelming.

In your own fight to do your best every day, family, friends, co-workers, subordinates, and bosses are good sources of support. In the unlikely event no one is available to support you, make finding a support team a priority. Enlist the help of a mentor at work. Join a group where people have similar interests and problems. Remember, the best athletes have coaches to help them maintain focus and improve. Don't try to "go it alone" or fail to hold up your end of the bargain by helping others as you've been helped.

Again, the five things necessary to do your best are **purpose, commitment, responsibility, flexibility,** and **support.** Leaders of integrity make certain they follow these steps and help their co-workers do the same—consistently.

"Doing my best" is often viewed as a product, but in reality it is a process. Winning athletes, artists, performers, managers, and business leaders continually focus on the process of doing their best. Consistently putting these five steps in practice sets them on an exciting path of growth, development, and success.

Continually look for new ways to accomplish your goals. Don't settle for the way you've always done it. The pace of change in today's world will make yesterday's solutions obsolete. Continuous improvement is a must for people and organizations who want to do their best. Consider new opportunities for learning and development as a way to keep your ideas fresh.

Since 1909, Boy Scouts have been pledging, "On my honor, I will do my best...." Scouts give their word to keep on doing their best. To be all that you want to be, you must do the same. If you practice doing your best, you will be your best. As Aristotle said, "We are what we repeatedly do. Excellence then, is not an act, but a habit."

Get in the habit of doing your best. Begin saying out loud, "I will do my best." My best what? My best work. My best to be a good spouse to my mate, parent to my kids, kid to my parents, neighbor to my neighbor, citizen to my country, employee to my organization, and leader to my employees.

Doing your best is a way of demonstrating commitment. Commitment is the single most important factor in becoming a long-term success in both your professional and personal life.

"ON MY HONOR, I WILL"

In the spaces below, list some commitments you wish to make in order to do your best.

On my honor, I will:

- _____
  _____
  _____

- _____
  _____
  _____

- _____
  _____
  _____

- _____
  _____
  _____

- _____
  _____
  _____

- _____
  _____
  _____
- _____
  _____
  _____

CHAPTER FOUR

On my honor, I will do my best:

TO DO MY DUTY

I slept and dreamed that life was beauty.
I woke—and found that life was duty.[9]

For many people, duty comes as a rude awakening—
usually sometime between puberty and adulthood. As
children, we often have duties *imposed* on us by others
and feel if we could only get out from under the
collective thumbs of parents and teachers, life would be
a beautiful adventure of fun and excitement. When the
day finally comes when we're on our own, we find we
have duties of our own—duties to our friends, to
ourselves, to our parents, to our peers.

We all have duties. Some duties are legal, such as our
duty to pay taxes, serve on juries, or serve in time of
national emergency. Other duties are moral, such as to

[9]"Beauty and Duty," *Ellen Sturgis Hooper (1816–1841).*

be a person of integrity, to provide and care for our families, to be all we can be, to pull our own weight. Our natural tendency is to do things that are fun, to "live for beauty." But when we become intellectually and morally aware, we wake and find that life is duty, which is another word for *responsibility*.

The awakening is cemented for most people when they move away from home for the first time. Despite other "duties" they may have experienced while growing up, nothing brings home the sense of duty and responsibility quite like making a car payment, paying the rent, buying groceries, paying for utilities, securing insurance, and filing tax returns.

Successful individuals understand that duty need not be drudgery. There can be tremendous freedom and happiness in doing your duty at home, in the community, and on the job.

So why do we have a shortage of responsibility takers? How can we cultivate a sense of duty in a world where society's feelings and actions were summed up one day when we heard an executive complain, "I think our number one problem is that nobody wants to take responsibility for anything—but don't quote me!"

The *easy answer* is that values are shifting, people are changing, and everyone is busy chasing the (once) almighty dollar. These things may be true, but they are often merely excuses for failure. We need solutions for success.

Today, America and American business have suffered because of a shortage of people willing to take responsibility. Managers and employees alike sometimes find it easier to hide behind the rules rather than accept responsibility. Some seem more interested in not losing a battle than in winning.

Bill Hampton, vice president of Michael Mead and

Associates, a pioneer in developing computerized route distribution systems for the food and beverage industry, observes, "There are companies that would spend ten thousand dollars to try to save a dime and wouldn't spend a dime to try and make ten thousand dollars!" These organizations and individuals have made the choice to do only the minimum required, to define duty and responsibility in the most narrow terms. Successful leaders and individuals, people who have made and will continue to make their mark on our lives, see duty differently. They see duty as the responsibility to work for everyone's benefit. In the organization, that means working to the benefit of:

Shareholders
Customers
Employees
Suppliers
Community.

In private life, that means working to the benefit of:

Family
Friends
Self.

As leaders, it is important not only that we do our duty but that we teach and inspire others to do theirs as well. John D. Rockefeller, Jr., speaking for the United Service Organization in 1941, said, "I believe that every right implies a responsibility; every opportunity, an obligation; every possession, a duty."

Robert E. Lee said, "Duty is the sublimest word in our language. Do your duty in all things. You cannot do more. You should never wish to do less."

THE IMPORTANCE OF MAKING CHOICES

As people of integrity, we do not get to choose whether or not to "do our duty"—we only get to choose *how* we will do our duty. If we have honor, we approach our duty with a high level of commitment. We are not content to just "do our job," we want to do more than our job. We not only want to do what's right, we want to do what *seems right*—even if we lose something in the process.

Case Study: Johnson & Johnson

A good example is the actions taken by Johnson & Johnson a few years ago when a maniac put poison in Tylenol capsules in the Chicago area and seven people died. No one attributed any blame to Johnson & Johnson, but the company voluntarily pulled the product off the shelves and kept it off until they had developed tamper-resistant packaging. Fortunately for Johnson & Johnson, they not only *did* the right thing, they were perceived as having done the right thing. The company suffered a short-term loss in profits, but their immediate sense of duty to their customers and the public resulted in a long-term increase in Tylenol's market share.

Johnson & Johnson didn't have to wonder how to react when the crisis came; they had a forty-year-old corporate credo, a philosophy that established the company's priorities and defined its responsibilities.

The credo states:

> **We believe our first responsibility** is to the doctors, nurses, and patients, to mothers and all others who use our products and services.

In meeting their needs everything we do must
be of high quality. We must constantly strive to
reduce our costs in order to maintain reasonable prices. Customers' orders must be serviced
promptly and accurately. Our suppliers and
distributors must have an opportunity to make
a fair profit.

We are responsible to our employees, the
men and women who work with us throughout the world. Everyone must be considered as
an individual. We must respect their dignity
and recognize their merit. They must have a
sense of security in their jobs. Compensation
must be fair and adequate, and working con-
ditions, clean, orderly, and safe. Employees
must feel free to make suggestions and complaints. There must be equal opportunity for
employment, development, and advancement
for those qualified. We must provide competent management, and their actions must be
just and ethical.

We are responsible to the communities in
which we live and work and to the world
community as well. We must be good citizens—
support good works and charities and bear
our fair share of taxes. We must encourage
civic improvements and better health and education. We must maintain in good order the
property we are privileged to use, protecting
the environment and natural resources.

Our final responsibility is to our stockholders. Business must make a sound profit. We
must experiment with new ideas. Research
must be carried on, innovative programs
developed, and mistakes paid for. New equip-

ment must be purchased, new facilities provided, and new products launched. When we
operate according to these principles, the stockholders should realize a fair return.

Did Johnson & Johnson "do their duty"? They went
above and beyond. They were up front with the media,
with the government, with the consumers—and both
the people and the press appreciated it. On February
21, 1986, the *Miami News* contrasted J&J's actions with
manufacturer A. H. Robins in these words. "By way
of odious comparison: In 1974, after three years and
2.86 million sales, A. H. Robins stopped selling its
Dalkon Shield intrauterine device. By then, the evidence was mounting that the shield was life-threatening
to users.

"Robins didn't recall the shield. Instead, it spent the
next ten years in court shuffling and ducking responsibility. Federal judge Miles Lord of Minneapolis called
the performance, 'corporate irresponsibility at its
meanest.'"

The *Miami News* article continued, "It [Johnson &
Johnson] lost $250 million in sales after the previous
cyanide scare, in 1982. But the company rebuilt its
market, at least partly because it treats people as human beings and not as contributors to its bottom line."
The article talked about J&J's move to New Brunswick,
New Jersey, and the fact that the company had poured
millions of dollars of its own money into helping the
city attract Urban Development Action Grant funds to
modernize and beautify the downtown, paid for training sessions in beautification and revitalization, etc.
They used this information to create another contrast
in corporate culture. Again, quoting the *Miami News*,
"While this was going on, only five miles away in . . .

Manville, N.J., the Manville Corp., the asbestos maker, faced an outburst of damage even bigger than the Dalkon Shield's. So Manville...filed for reorganization under Chapter 11 of the bankruptcy laws....Federal judge Jerome H. Sarokin of Newark says Manville 'manipulated the judicial system so as to delay to thousands of claimants and deny completely to some their day in court to present asbestos-related injuries.'"

The article concludes, "J&J is in business to make money. It has done that very well. But when the going gets tough, the corporation gets human, and that makes it something special in the...business world."

The lesson from J&J is clear: If you do what is right, people will eventually notice it. If others don't do what is right—well, then you'll look all the better for the comparison.

Case Study: National Gypsum Company

In the mid 1970s, National Gypsum Company, the second-largest supplier of wallboard in North America, forecast that the coming building boom would be centered in the South. Therefore, they began investigating the possibility of moving the headquarters for the Gold Bond wallboard division from Buffalo, New York, to a more centrally located city in their primary growth market.

When the announcement of a site selection was made, the press in Buffalo responded negatively, stating that the announcement was a new low in corporate relations, despite the company's obvious attempt to make the best of a difficult decision. The company made every effort to balance the needs of all parties concerned. National did their duty to shareholders by

making a good business decision. They did their duty
to customers by positioning the company to offer quality products at a reasonable price (which can only be
done by being close to markets). They did their duty to
suppliers, by remaining in business so commerce could
continue. They did their duty to employees, moving
the vast majority to Charlotte, assigning some to other
operations, and allowing still others to take early
retirement. A small minority of employees held positions
not continued, and they were paid liberal retirement
benefits.

There are times, of course, when duty takes you
through a veritable mine field of conflicting wants and
needs. A good case in point was the LBO (leveraged
buy out) of National Gypsum Company in 1986. At
that time, National Gypsum produced not only wallboard, but floor covering, glass, and other related
home building and remodeling products. These are all
commodities driven by the law of supply and demand,
and the company was experiencing good sales, good
profits, and had a long history of paying good dividends to shareholders. However, price/earning multi-
ples were low by NYSE standards, which brought the
company to the attention of corporate raiders.

In early November 1985, rumors were mounting of a
hostile takeover of National Gypsum Company by the
Belzberg family of Canada. The company had earlier
resisted takeover attempts by both Victor Posner and
Louisiana-Pacific. Since hostile takeovers are historically made by leveraging the future of the company to
cover the debt incurred, John P. Hayes, CEO of National Gypsum, had to face the problem of ensuring
that shareholders received the greatest value possible
for their investment while also preserving the company's long-term viability.

Hayes said, "There were more than economic considerations involved in our decision. Many people had spent virtually all their working lives with National Gypsum Company. Our associates and customers had become our friends as well. An unfriendly takeover would have had a tremendous negative impact on the company and our customers, and the futures of our employees would have been severely threatened."

On November 25, 1985, a management-led investor group, known as Aancor Holdings, Inc., initiated an offer to National Gypsum shareholders for $40.50 cash and $17 face value of 15½ percent redeemable discount debentures. The value of this offer was significantly greater than the highest market value ever attained by the company's common stock.[10]

To protect shareholders' interests, the board of directors created a fairness committee that hired Salomon Brothers and Dillon Reed to render fairness opinions regarding the offer. On January 7, 1986, the investor group proposed a revised merger proposal of $41 in cash and $17 in debentures, which received the approval of National's board of directors, with the final decision to be made by shareholders at the April 10 meeting.

For three months, both the financial community and the media felt the management-led leveraged buy out was a "done deal." Then at 3:25 P.M. on April 8, 1986, the phone on John Hayes's desk rang. Sanford Sigoloff, chairman of Wickes, came on the line and said they were putting out a press release at that time indicating they were going to make a tender offer for all the stock of National Gypsum at $54 a share.

[10]Marc Bockmon, *Turning Points: The National Gypsum Story,* Taylor Publishing, 1990.

The reasoning was that an upturn in the building business made the company potentially more valuable. Still, as Jack Hayes recalls, "I couldn't have been more surprised. First of all, Wickes was a large customer of ours. I felt an acquisition by Wickes would alienate many of National Gypsum's customers. On top of that, Wickes had just come out of bankruptcy and was a most unlikely suitor. I shared this with Sandy, and he indicated it was strictly a financial deal and shouldn't affect the marketing operations of the business. Again, I was surprised and somewhat startled to hear he didn't think a financial deal of this magnitude would affect marketing."

The *easy* road for National's management would have been to acquiesce to Wickes's demands. The shareholders would have received more for the stock than it had ever sold for. National Gypsum's top management was nearing retirement age, had a large block of stock, and there must have been some thought about "taking the money and running." Management, however, agonized over their duty not only to shareholders, but to customers, employees, suppliers, and the communities they served.

In the end, management fought the hostile takeover and won. True, in so doing, they drove up the debt of the company, effectively mortgaging the future. True, it meant divesting some divisions. "Well," you may well ask, "then what was the purpose of fighting the takeover?"

The leader's duty is to balance the long-term needs of all constituencies. To mortgage the long-term needs of customers, employees, suppliers, and communities for the immediate return to shareholders ultimately affects the long-term viability of each shareholder's investment. Organizations that fail to do their duty to all groups eventually corrupt their ability to effectively work with any group.

As Allan V. Cecil, PR director of National Gypsum, explains, "The main thing was that the company had been saved, jobs and benefits for workers were secure, and shareholders and customers had benefited. In fact, an investor that had purchased a thousand shares of National Gypsum common stock on April 29, 1985, would have seen a 139 percent increase a year later!"

Since that time, a downturn in building starts coupled with the high cost of borrowed money has forced National Gypsum Company into Chapter 11. While the eventual outcome remains to be seen, discussions with management at the company indicate they feel this is a *liquidity* problem and not an *ethical* problem—and that all creditors and suppliers will be dealt with fairly and equitably.

DO DUTIES EVER CONFLICT?

As the previous example shows, doing your duty doesn't always make you popular—or guarantee instant success. It does, however, produce positive long-term benefits. Earlier we mentioned Howard Putnam and the initial Braniff bankruptcy. The result of Putnam's sense of duty was that Braniff emerged from bankruptcy without a single shareholder lawsuit. On the personal level, former employees were known to still carry handwritten notes received from Putnam years afterward. Duty may have its costs in the short term, but it reaps incredible rewards over the long haul.

What do you do if you are caught in a situation where, in spite of your efforts to do your duty, you're perceived as derelict? Perhaps just follow the advice of

French playwright Pierre Corneille (1606–1684), "Do your duty and leave the rest to heaven."

As leaders we often have several paths of duty to tread. Those paths may diverge, but we do not believe they have to conflict.

On the surface, there may appear to be a conflict among paths because each group with whom we deal has a different need. On closer examination, however, we usually find that the paths of duty are intertwined and meeting one need helps meet others. When Charles E. Wilson, president of General Motors, was nominated by President Eisenhower as secretary of defense in 1953, Senator Richard Russell asked him if he would be willing, if necessary, to make a decision unfavorable to General Motors. Wilson said, "What's good for the country is good for General Motors, and vice versa." That is often the way it is with our duties, they are so intertwined and interdependent that whatever helps or hurts one helps or hurts all.

What do **shareholders** need? A high rate of return on their investment or, failing that, a *secure* investment.

What do **customers** need? Good, dependable products and services that offer *value*.

What do **employees** need? Secure employment, competitive pay and benefits, a sense of corporate and self worth.

What do **suppliers** need? They want a customer who pays a fair price on time and who considers them a partner in profit, a member of the team.

What does the **community** need? They want good corporate citizens who will provide jobs and opportunities for their people as well as expand the tax base so they can afford to provide good schools, streets, and services.

As a leader faced with these divergent needs, you

can't "do your duty" to any group without doing your duty to the others! If you meet the needs of shareholders but not of employees, you have strikes. If you meet the needs of employees but not shareholders, they dump your stock on the market. If you don't meet the needs of your customers, then everyone is out of a job. *Your duty then lies in doing your best for all of them.* (No one ever said duty was easy!)

Case Study: The Development of the Pulse Furnace at Lennox

In 1975, representatives of the American Gas Association's Gas Research Institute demonstrated to furnace manufacturers a new process they had developed for a pulse combustion furnace. Pulse combustion offered the potential of not only being a highly efficient heating system but also adding safety and life to the heat exchanger—the most expensive component of a home heating system.

At the time, traditional furnaces were 55 to 56 percent efficient, and there seemed to be a barrier on efficiency. If the air were recirculated through the system to extract extra heat, caustic chemicals naturally present in home air condensed and would quickly begin eating into the metal in the heat exchanger. Any savings the homeowner would gain in fuel efficiency were more than "eaten up" by the cost of heat exchanger replacements. The Pulse offered the potential of high efficiency without having to recirculate flue gases.

The downside was that the Pulse prototype was the size of an office, and home furnaces are made to fit into a rather small closet. To perfect and miniaturize the prototype would require years of work and millions of dollars. Since natural gas was cheap, there was no evidence that consumers would pay a premium price for a premium unit. As one competitor remarked, "Using a Pulse system for heating is like making an apple box out of a desk—you can do it, but it isn't cost efficient."

Lennox Industries, one of the three largest heating and air-conditioning equipment manufacturers in North America, had a history of commitment to providing the most dependable, highest quality heating, ventilating, and air-conditioning equipment in the world. It was a commitment that was first made in 1885 when Dave Lennox made the world's first steel furnace. Yet, in a highly competitive marketplace, was Lennox willing to risk the future of the company on a new technology that people might not want anyway?

Ray Robbins, Chairman Emeritus of parent company Lennox International, was president when the go/no go decision was being made on the Pulse furnace. He recalls, "We had a duty to our shareholders, our customers, our employees, our suppliers, and the communities where we work and live. Our first obligation was *corporate survival—to be there in the future*. Yet we were well aware of John Paul Jones's admonition that 'He who will not risk, cannot win.' We had a reputation as an industry leader, and that reputation could only be kept if we were willing to take the inherent risks involved in leadership. Besides, we felt that the cost of natural gas was *unnaturally low*—and it wouldn't take much of a rise in cost to make upgrading to a Pulse furnace a better investment than CD's or money market accounts.

"After a lot of study, we made an executive decision to explore Pulse technology and begin developing a market for high-efficiency heating products while we worked. However, since others were involved, we went to the shareholders, told them what the potential risks and profits were, and got their blessings to go ahead."

Five years after Lennox accepted the challenge, the first twenty units went into field testing in homes in Chicago, Minneapolis, and Cleveland. The first units were every bit as efficient as R&D had promised. One gas meter man, who knew nothing of the test, told a homeowner with a Pulse furnace, "You must have been gone last month—your fuel bill is half what it should have been!"

In addition to efficiency, the early Pulse units verified the predictions about longevity. Tests showed that Pulse heat exchangers with the equivalent of twenty years worth of use still looked brand-new. The only initial problem was that the Pulse furnaces were slightly noisier than ordinary furnaces. It took an additional two years to solve that problem, and only then did Lennox feel the product was ready to introduce to dealers and the public.

The rest, as they say, is history. The Pulse furnace started the high-efficiency industry, and Lennox became the first manufacturer to offer a lifetime warranty on a heat exchanger. Everyone benefited because the Pulse made the heating market bigger since, for the first time, it made sense to replace a *working furnace*. As a result, customers saved money, shareholders made money, suppliers had a bigger customer, and the communities where Lennox plants were located had a bigger employer.

What would have happened if Lennox management had only looked at *part of their duty*? What would have been the result if duty to shareholders to minimize risk had been their primary consideration? What would have happened if they'd worried only about suppliers of current parts? If they'd only focused on the needs of the independent dealers, who are their customers? Lennox learned a lesson we all need to remember: *Duty requires balancing the needs of each group in order to better meet the needs of everyone.*

INTERACTIVE EXERCISE

The leader who focuses all of his/her attention on only one area risks the disruption of relations with the others. If shareholders and stakeholders are ignored, they will cease to support the organization. If employees are ignored, lower productivity may result. If suppliers are ignored, it becomes difficult to secure the resources the organization needs to operate. If the community is ignored, the loss of support influences all other areas.

Let's assume that you are in charge of your organization. What is your "duty" to the following groups and how would you demonstrate that duty?

GROUP: SHAREHOLDERS
DUTY: _____

_____

_____

ACTION YOU WOULD TAKE: _____

_____

_____

GROUP: CUSTOMERS
DUTY: _____

_____

_____

ACTION YOU WOULD TAKE: _____

_____

_____

GROUP: EMPLOYEES
DUTY: _____

_____

ACTION YOU WOULD TAKE: _____

_____

_____

GROUP: SUPPLIERS
DUTY: _____

_____

ACTION YOU WOULD TAKE: _____

_____

_____

GROUP: COMMUNITY
DUTY: _____

_____

ACTION YOU WOULD TAKE: _____

_____

_____

DUTY CALLS FROM MANY DIRECTIONS

In the previous exercise, we looked at our duties to
those with whom we work. We have other duties as
well. We have duties to our family, our friends, and to
ourselves. The balance required of successful leaders

extends beyond work into all other areas of life. Without that balance, we lose the perspective that allows us to see the "big picture" of life. The massive generators that supply our electricity have to receive preventive maintenance occasionally. Taking a day off to fish, play golf, have a family outing, or spend time with friends can enable us to "do our duty" more effectively and efficiently.

In the spaces below, write down your duty to those outside the organization and the actions you will take to more effectively live up to that responsibility.

GROUP: FAMILY
DUTY: _____
_____
_____
ACTION I WILL TAKE: _____
_____
_____

GROUP: FRIENDS
DUTY: _____
_____
_____
ACTION I WILL TAKE: _____
_____
_____

GROUP: MYSELF
DUTY: _____
_____
_____
ACTION I WILL TAKE: _____
_____
_____

A call to duty is not inborn, it is developed. We do our duty, even when we would sometimes rather not because we have either been trained or have trained ourselves. We do our duty because we are committed to succeed and to help others succeed. We do our duty because we are people of honor.

Eddie Rickenbacker was a champion auto racer, but when World War I began, his sense of duty caused him to leave that behind and join the army, where he became America's leading air ace. In 1938, he became president of Eastern Air Lines. During World War II, he was on an inspection trip for Secretary of War Stimson and was forced down in the Pacific, where he drifted on a rubber raft for twenty-four days before being rescued. After the war, he returned to full-time duties at Eastern and served as president until 1959, when he became chairman of the board. He did his duty as a young man, as an elderly man, and all the days of his life. Why? Where did he learn his doctrine of duty? The answer may surprise you.

Rickenbacker says, "My first job was as important as any I ever had. It was my initiation into a man's world. Being a newsboy taught me the meaning of duty, and without a sense of duty a man is nothing." Many young people today don't consider a paper route very important— yet one of the greatest men of our time says it was the most important thing in developing his sense of duty. He learned to make commitments and keep them. He learned to depend on himself—and to make himself dependable. The things he learned peddling his papers lasted a lifetime.

Earlier in this chapter, we raised a question: "How can we cultivate a sense of duty in a world where it appears that no one is willing to accept responsibility for anything?" The best way is by our own example, by letting others see how important duty is to us. Duty and responsibility can be learned the way anything is learned: by observation, study, and practice. Scouts learn about duty from their Scoutmaster, from older Scouts, from their parents, and their peers. The people we lead learn from us. But where do leaders learn about duty? Here are a few ideas on how you can enhance your commitment to "do your duty."

- Find a friend, co-worker, or boss who exhibits a strong sense of duty. Watch how that individual responds to the challenges of balancing all of life's duties. Ask that individual for feedback when you face the challenges associated with doing your duty.
- Look for positive examples from history. Find out all you can about the heroes or heroines you chose. Establish them as your personal "board of advisors" and ask yourself, "How would that person have responded in this situation?"
- Identify people in your community or your profession to serve as mentors. Many of the leaders in your community or profession are willing to invest time in people they see are committed to personal improvement and service. However, if you approach one of these people, make certain you are prepared to use their time wisely. They, in all probability, will be giving up something to help you. Make sure their efforts are worthwhile.
- Put yourself in situations where you must do your duty on a regular basis. Commit to helping some individual or group. Make a special effort to help someone else learn the importance of doing their duty. Begin talking with your employees or peers about the importance of duty. Nothing moves us to

action like the pressure of knowing others are watching our behavior.

Daniel Webster said, "A sense of duty pursues us ever. It is omnipresent, like the Deity. If we take to ourselves the wings of the morning and dwell in the uttermost parts of the sea, duty performed or duty violated is still with us, for our happiness or our misery. If we say the darkness shall cover us, in the darkness, as in the light our obligations are yet with us."

We do not get to decide whether or not to have duties. Duties come with the territory. Our only choice is how we choose to do our duty. Our professional and our personal lives hang on how wisely we choose. How will *you* choose?

"ON MY HONOR, I WILL"

In the spaces below, list the commitments you wish to make regarding your duty.

On my honor, I will:

- _____
  _____
  _____

- _____
  _____
  _____

- _____
  _____
  _____

- _____
  _____
  _____

- _____
  _____
  _____

CHAPTER FIVE

On my honor, I will do my best:
1. To do my duty

TO GOD AND MY COUNTRY

A Scout's first duty is to God and country. Our relationship to our God defines our relationship to others, just as our relationship to our country defines the boundaries of our identity and loyalty. When the Scout Oath was written, most Americans had a common concept of God, based on Judeo-Christian roots. Beliefs vary, and Scouting takes the differences into account in today's more pluralistic society. Yet, the belief that we are accountable for our actions toward others is a basic religious concept.

Moses handed down the principles of accountability to the children of Israel in the form of the Ten Commandments. Christ proclaimed them to his followers by saying that love for one another was the only way for people to know that they were his disciples. Buddha, Confucius, and Aristotle also have their teachings grounded in the belief that we are accountable for our actions. The belief is best described in the Golden Rule: "Do unto others as you would have them do unto you."[11] This belief forms the underpinning of integrity and morality in our dealing with others. It is the foundation of our ethical and legal system, for without the concept of "right and wrong" there would be no basis for common guidelines. The belief that lying, cheating, stealing, and murder are morally wrong led to the creation of laws against them.

Some would tell us that such moral underpinnings are out of step with today's society. There are those who act as if they believe that "greed is good," that the Golden Rule should read "Do unto others before they do unto you," and that you should "look out for number one." Those who follow these principles rarely succeed long-term. Their downfall is based on the shortsighted view that you can continually treat people unfairly and with disrespect and expect them to keep doing business with you.

In truth, the opposite occurs. Long-term successes in business and life follow a moral code defined by the Golden Rule. This code defines their relationship to their higher calling, whether it be religious or moral, by defining their relationship to others through action.

Likewise, our duty to country provides and identifies a sense of belonging necessary for our survival and success. Technology, cooperation among nations, and world economics have blurred the lines of individual countries. We now operate as a part of the global market, dealing with a number of other trading part-

[11]Paraphrased from Luke 6:31.

ners. Technology allows a business in New York to be
linked directly and simultaneously with Tokyo, Berlin,
Moscow, Mexico City, and Montreal. Yet, a sense of
identity and belonging still exists. Travelers worldwide
still identify themselves by their country of origin when
visiting a foreign nation.

The Boy Scouts in 1911 saw duty to country as an
obligation to fight and protect it from outside aggres-
sors, to vote, serve on juries, take part in the governing
process and issues of the day, and to build strong
families and communities. Those needs still exist today.
In fact, the need has increased. As our country has
grown and changed we have seen example after example of groups and individuals violating its laws and
becoming irresponsible in their service. Today, many
who are called for jury duty walk into court with every
possible excuse not to serve. Others feel compelled to
get out of jury duty because their employer doesn't pay
them if they are not at work. Many of the same people
later bemoan the rise of crime in the streets.

Complaining about the actions of our elected leaders
has become a national pastime, but voter apathy remains high. The list could go on and on and on of
people showing disrespect for their duty to their country and complaining because things are not going as
they would have them.

If we thumb our noses at our moral duty to others
and our duty to country, we should not be surprised by
people around us not meeting theirs. Society's norms
are established by individuals like us getting involved.
C. S. Lewis observed, "We laugh at honor and are
surprised to find there are traitors in our midst." The
many treason cases that have come to light would
indicate that Professor Lewis was right. But more important, Lewis was telling us that unless individuals

become active in fulfilling their duty to God and country, we should not be surprised when our country and its people do not make good decisions and maintain moral behavior. The bad examples are well reported in the press. Fortunately, there is no shortage of good examples of businesses and business leaders who honor their God and their country, and by doing so, achieve greater success. Let's look at some of them.

Case Study: The Dr Pepper Company

W. W. "Foots" Clements, chairman emeritus of the Dr Pepper Company, learned the value of honor and commitment to God and country at home and as a Boy Scout. Growing up in rural Alabama, he learned to pull his weight at an early age. His first job was carrying lunches to farm workers, and when he was big enough, he tended turkeys, chopped weeds, and hoed cotton. His first work "for pay" was trapping opossums, selling their skins for $1.25. When he was eleven, he took a weekend job working in a combination grocery store and gristmill. As he grew older he hauled lumber, ran a newspaper route, and sold magazines. By the time he was in high school, he was working as a part-time butcher.

In 1935, at the age of twenty-one, "Foots" took a job as a route salesman for the Dr Pepper Bottling Company in Tuscaloosa, Alabama, at $10 a week. In 1942, he was hired by the Dr Pepper Company itself as a zone manager. By 1967, he was executive vice president and a director. Two years later, he became president and chief operating officer, and CEO the following year. In 1980, he became chairman of the board, becoming chairman emeritus in 1986.

During Clements's years at the helm of Dr Pepper, he was able to transform this small, regional soft drink into the number three soft drink in America. While this kind of drive and determination would consume all the resources of most men, Clements accomplished it in addition to a full load in a host of civic and outside business responsibilities. He served as a director of banks, life insurance companies, colleges, hospitals, and such organizations as the Laymen's National Bible Committee, Better Business Bureau, American Red Cross, The Salvation Army, U.S.O., and the Circle Ten Council of the Boy Scouts, to name a few. Asked if he ever got tired, he laughed. "Sure, there has been a lifetime of long days and long weeks. But, the things I did for God, and country, and community made me a better person. Everything I did ultimately helped me in my job." W. W. Clements not only has a Horatio Alger success story, he is a recipient of the Horatio Alger award for his "bootstrap" rise from poverty to success.

"Foots" has given away thousands of marbles with the Golden Rule written on them. Skeptics ask, "Can you build a competitive business on the Golden Rule?" He always answers, "You cannot build a business that will last except by practicing the Golden Rule. Our people at Dr Pepper are taught this. It is our foundation." "Foots" feels if you have ability and follow the Golden Rule, you'll succeed. As he told the students at Tuscaloosa County High School on Horatio Alger Day, March 6, 1990, "Horatio Alger members are people who recognize and understand that you can't do it alone...we are motivated to put something back into the system that has been so good to us—not just our money, but our time and effort to help others understand the abundant opportunities that exist in our country.... I hope you will be convinced that if I made it, anyone can make it, if they work hard and follow the Golden Rule."

Case Study: Gerber Baby Foods

On July 28, 1990, the Associated Press ran the following story:

Raymond Dunn, Jr., turned 16 Tuesday, but the profoundly retarded birthday boy feasted not on cake, to which he is allergic, but on the day's greatest gift: the bland, brown infant formula that keeps him alive.

Gerber Products Co., which stopped making the meat-based formula in 1985, resumed production two months ago after Raymond's doctors said that he would die without it. Gerber employees volunteered to make a batch on their own time, and on June 26 the Dunns received a two-year supply free of charge.

"Gerber says, 'Babies are our business,' but Raymond is their business too," said Carol Dunn, who spent five years trying to get the company to retool for a market of one. When Gerber decided to drop the product five years ago, Mrs. Dunn was unable to find or create any substitute that did not make Raymond sick. Frantic, she hunted down every can she could find, and Gerber kept passing along its own backlog. By July 1988, Gerber ran out of MBF, leaving Raymond with less that two years' supply.

Supported by the State Association for Retarded Children, Mrs. Dunn begged Gerber to make more MBF and began a mail campaign asking others to pressure the company. Finally, the company's research director consented. Meanwhile, at Gerber, volunteers in the research division put their own projects on hold, hauled out old equipment, and devoted seven thousand square feet and several days of production space and time to Raymond's supply of MBF. It arrived in Yankee Lake (NY) in time. The Dunns had about two dozen cans of the old formula, enough to last through the end of July.

Why would a company and its employees go to so much trouble for a market of one? The obvious answer was that they cared—really cared. To skeptics that might counter with, "But they got a lot of good publicity out of it!" we respond, "So? What's wrong with getting credit for a good deed?"

WHY DO WE DO WHAT WE DO?

As "Foots" Clements observed, "Not only do we have a responsibility to our business, our employees, and the people we serve, but also to our system, our home and to God." Our responsibility to a higher calling, be it religious or moral, assumes that the actions we take to help others are taken because we want to, not because we have to or expect recognition.

Truly successful people, leaders, and organizations recognize this and act accordingly. Their decision to give back to society and practice the Golden Rule is based on an internal motivation. They expect little in return except the satisfaction of seeing others have the opportunity to experience success. In the Old Testament story Cain asked the Lord, "Am I my brother's keeper?" The answer was "Yes!" We all have a responsibility to be involved in the social issues of the day. It makes for good business because it makes for good people.

Case Study: Golden Rule Life Insurance Company

Golden Rule Life Insurance Company began in 1940 with a pledge to follow the Golden Rule with all their business dealings. Today, they have $5.9 billion of insurance in force, and premium income for 1990 was $450 million. We asked Richard Merrill, vice president of financial products, if the company was committed to that rule regardless of the consequences. He laughed and said, "Of course we are."

Pressed for an example, he said, "Shortly after I came here in 1984, we were marketing a single premium whole life product that offered unusual advantages for the clients of insurance brokers. Prior to changes in the tax law in 1988, insurance companies had almost $40 billion worth of this product in force.

"Even though we were early into the market and had a chance to capture a major market share, our products had one distinction from the others. The competitors' products advertised their policy as having "no insurance charges," which meant if you put $25,000 into the policy, the computer illustration showed money growing, for example, at a net 9 percent interest rate with no charges against it.

"By contrast, our product showed a 10 percent interest rate and an insurance charge of 1 percent. Although the bottom line return to the customer was the same, we felt telling the *whole truth* made it clear that the customer was paying for insurance. We felt this was important, because as people get older, the insurance charges increase, and we wanted people to understand this fully going in."

Merrill added, "I have to admit, as a product manager whose bonus was based on production, my natural inclination was to join the herd and do it the way everyone else did. I spoke to our CEO, J. Patrick Rooney, about it, and he was adamant that we follow the Golden Rule. He merely pointed to the company's mission statement, which says: '*At Golden Rule, we choose to be ethical because it is right, not because it is good business practice. We value hard work and promptness, and we are committed to doing things right. We want our products to provide our customers with the best long-term value in the marketplace.*'

"As a result, our sales were sluggish—so there was a very big price to pay for doing the right thing. However, a change in the tax-change law eventually killed the product line for everyone. When that happened, nearly all our competitors decreased the interest rate credited to the policies to offset the hidden insurance costs. Today, a lot of our business comes from customers of those policies who liked our "tell it like it is" approach, plus quite a few who bought competitors' products and found it was really as we said it was. So, in the long run, doing the honorable thing, the right thing, and following the Golden Rule, pays off."

WE ARE ACCOUNTABLE TO COUNTRY

In his inaugural address, President John F. Kennedy observed, "To whom much is given, much is required. And when at some future date the high court of history sits in judgment on each of us, recording whether in our brief span of service we fulfilled our responsibilities to the state, our success or failure, in whatever office we hold, will be measured by the answers to four questions: First, were we truly men of courage? Second, were we truly men of judgment? Third, were we truly men of integrity? Finally, were we truly men of dedication?"

Noble words for a president, but what do they mean for those of us who are just "average citizens?" How do we "do our duty" to our country? One way is active participation. Our duty to our country includes:

Paying our taxes
Serving on juries
Obeying the laws
Voting
Involvement in schools, education, and social issues
Serving in the armed forces when necessary
Involvement in building strong families and communities.

In a very real sense, doing our duty to our country is doing our duty to ourselves. Since our country provides us with safety and security, doing our duty is in our own best interest. We must help the "ship of state" sail on, because if the ship sinks, all the passengers are in peril.

The day after World War II began, Melvin Baker, president of National Gypsum Company, sent a telegram to War Secretary Henry Stimson that said, "The management of this corporation believes that business should go all out for quick, decisive victory...and to this end, the company's resources, technical knowledge and the production at its twenty-one plants are at your disposal." The government was quick to take Baker up on the offer and sent a team of attorneys to work out the details with the company's attorneys. As the haggling over the details dragged on, Baker stood up and said, "There's a war on. Let's forget about dotting the *i*'s. We're in this thing together!" Both sets of attorneys were startled into silence for a moment, then they laughed and quickly signed the necessary papers.

Baker's statement is still appropriate today. We are engaged in a war, fighting such enemies as homelessness, poverty, hunger, illiteracy, discrimination, substance addiction, and a host of other problems that threaten to sink the ship of state. Our duty to country is a duty to ourselves. Ultimately, everyone's interest is best served when the needs of each individual are met.

MY COUNTRY AND THE WORLD

Today, we live in a global village, and we must both coexist and compete with the world. An individual's first responsibility is to family and friends, then their own community and country. However, responsibility must extend to the rest of the world. As fellow travelers on spaceship Earth, we share a common destiny, just as if we were passengers on the same steamship. If the bow of a ship sinks, the stern follows. If the bow of a ship sails safely into port, the stern does, too.

John Donne, in his book *Devotions*, published in 1624, perhaps said it best:

No man is an island, entire of itself; every man is a piece of the continent, a part of the main; if a clod be washed away by the sea, Europe is the less, as well as if promontory were, as well as if a manor of thy friends or of thine own were; any man's death diminishes me, because I am involved in mankind; and therefore never send to know for whom the bell tolls; it tolls for thee.

It is easy to take the advantage of country for granted. Sometimes the spectacular can become almost commonplace, and it is only when we return after a long absence that we can really understand what country means to us. Sometimes it is easier to see it through the eyes of another.

When Hue Cao fled Vietnam with her mother and two brothers in 1979, she spoke no English. Yet, in 1986, she won a state-sponsored essay contest on "What the Statue of Liberty Means to Me." Her essay said, in part, "We wanted to live in America, a land where there is liberty and justice. Every time we saw a picture of the Statue of Liberty, my mother would tell us *she* is America. America is a place that lends a hand to those in need. The Americans care for all people, from hopeless to homeless."

There is a lot of truth in Hue Cao's words—Americans care. No country has ever approached the generosity of America. No nation in history has matched us either in total or per capita giving. We give as individuals. We give as corporations. We give as a country. Caring and sharing are part of our national heritage. It was a major factor in the survival of the early settlers, and it must continue today both here and abroad.

It is easy to feel hopeless about the challenges that

exist in the world. There are so many staggering needs. Many feel that there is little use. After all, what can one person do?

Syndicated columnist George Will says, "Over and over, we hear people ask, 'What can I do—I'm only one person?' That's a nonquestion, since you can never be more than one person!" None of us is able to do everything, but each of us is able to do something to make this a better world; it is our duty. C. S. Lewis wrote, "We have no right to happiness. We have only an obligation to do our duty." Writer Cal Thomas says, "It is in doing that duty that ultimate happiness is to be found." History tells us that it is often a mistake to underestimate the power of one individual committed to a specific goal. Our next case study is an excellent example of what we mean.

Case Study: The Body Shop

Anita Roddick is an entrepreneur who places a high value on integrity, duty, and concern for the welfare of others. In 1976, she was an English homemaker with two young daughters. But she had an idea for a store that would feature natural body products. She opened her first store with a $6,400 loan. Ten months later, she had two. The Body Shop operates today in thirty-nine countries and has annual sales of over $140 million.

How did she do it? By offering good products that are gentle on the skin and gentle on the environment. By doing away with sales hype and merely explaining what the products do. By taking care of customers, employees, and the environment.

Without traditional advertising, the Body Shop has become successful in a highly competitive business. It relies on word-of-mouth from satisfied customers and the high visibility of their stores. Once inside, there's plenty of information in print and on video about the products, and the staff knows the products they sell. Salespeople receive training in areas such as product knowledge, maintaining clean, attractive stores and displays, and treating customers courteously. The goal is to make them better people who can help customers rather than better salespeople.

The Body Shop is interested in doing more than protecting the environment with its products. It is interested in protecting the environment, period. The company has made saving the Brazilian rain forest a major issue and contributed hundreds of thousands of dollars to aid in the project. In addition, they have produced videotapes, posters, and T-shirts to bring the issue to the people. The basic message is "The Indians are the custodians of the rain forests, the rain forests are the lungs of the world, if they die, we all die."

The Body Shop is interested not only in saving the rain forest in Brazil but also looks for ways to help closer to home. Under its Trade Not Aid program, the Body Shop built a soap factory in an area in Glasgow, Scotland, where some people have been unemployed for ten years. The company's feeling was as long as it's going to build a plant, it might as well put it where it'll do the most good!

Speaking of doing the most good, Body Shop employees are expected to work on a community project for at least an hour a week. Thus, the Body Shop's giving spirit is transformed into community action. Expecting work on a community project might sound dictatorial except for one thing—employees are paid for their efforts.

To the detractors who argue, "Well, they get a lot of favorable publicity for doing good things," we say, "Terrific!" There are so many examples of organizations and people who only take from society and never give back, we are glad the groups and individuals mentioned here are receiving recognition. The only thing that would be better is a society where giving back is so common that no one thinks such an act is deserving of public recognition. For those waiting for a ground swell before they take up their favorite cause, there is good news.

We are more likely than ever before to find other hands reaching out to help. We have seen global cooperation on whaling, acid rain, ozone depletion, reduction of the rain forests, and in quarantining aggressor nations. As more and more people, organizations, and countries come to realize that we are all passengers on the same ship, we can expect to see more and more willing to work together to "do their duty" in the future.

Whether it is leading to clean up pollution, provide educational opportunities for those poorly served by the "system," ensure food and shelter for the homeless, or one of many other "causes" that deserve attention, our duty is the same—to give back and to follow the Golden Rule in all our actions.

"ON MY HONOR, I WILL"

In the space below, list the commitments you wish to make to follow the Golden Rule and give back to society.

On my honor, I will:

- _____
  _____
  _____

- _____
  _____
  _____

- _____
  _____
  _____

- _____
  _____
  _____

- _____
  _____
  _____

CHAPTER SIX

On my honor, I will do my best:
1. To do my duty to God and my country, and

TO OBEY THE SCOUT LAW*

Laws are the rules and regulations that enable us to live together in harmony and peace. They are also the guidelines and principles that, if followed, will produce consistent results.

Most people, for instance, look at laws as the rules by which we should live. They look at the fifty-five mph speed limit on noninterstate U.S. highways as a rule that governs the way they drive. They view the laws regarding personal conduct as the boundaries by which people everywhere live in harmony. Frost said, "Good fences make good neighbors." Laws, if you will, are the

*A Scout is trustworthy, loyal, helpful, friendly, courteous, kind, obedient, cheerful, thrifty, brave, clean, reverent.

"good fences" that separate our rights from our neighbor's rights and permit us all to live in relative harmony. Laws in societies everywhere establish the foundation for the society's actions.

In a simpler time, people followed the principles embodied in the Scout Law without questioning why. Those few people who didn't follow the law were ostracized or at least held in contempt. But, those days are gone, and times today are different and more complex. Today, we sometimes see those who violate the principles of integrity honored as if bad were good and right were wrong. When we see such things, it's logical to ask, "Why would anyone in today's competitive environment want to follow such strong principles?" It's a good question and, fortunately, there's a good answer. Leaders of integrity know that by following these principles, their organizations will reap multiplied results. In return for their efforts, they receive results such as:

Increased loyalty from employees and customers
Word-of-mouth advertising
Fewer people problems
Safer work environments
Increased profits
Less personal stress
Increased personal satisfaction and perspective.

It almost sounds too easy, doesn't it? Obey a few principles that have been around forever and reap incredible results. Conventional wisdom tells us that anything that sounds too good to be true probably *is* too good to be true. Are we countering conventional wisdom? Absolutely not.

Like the Ten commandments, the Magna Charta,

and the Bill of Rights, which forms the first ten amendments of the U.S. Constitution, the Scout Law is based on principles that work. Many good examples are given in this book—hundreds more could be given. The principle is that you reap what you sow. It applies to every industry, every business, every life. What goes in will, in time, come out—multiplied.

Case Study: XYZ Manufacturing

Several years ago a midwestern manufacturing company decided to implement a Values Program. The program's stated purpose was to send a clear message to customers, employees, suppliers, and the community that XYZ Manufacturing was trustworthy. The senior management team knew and believed that the company's image among customers, suppliers, and the community depended on the behavior of the organization's employees. The senior managers also knew that their trust, loyalty, respect, and credibility were in short supply with employees. Years before, there had been a bitter strike, and the wounds had never completely healed. Employees felt betrayed and mistreated. Their feelings were transmitted to the community and to customers.

XYZ Manufacturing adopted several strategies to implement their Values Program. They posted plaques, printed cards for wallets, and stickers for hard hats. They mailed letters to every home and placed value-oriented articles in all the local papers. "Values" was the subject of every speech and every company newsletter. Everything that could be done to carry out the new Values Program was done...except one—managers did not change the way they managed.

XYZ forgot the basic premise of change: the main thing is to make the main thing the main thing. They were trying to put a Band-Aid on a cancer and overcome fifty years of problems with a public relations campaign. Management wasn't trying to "pull a fast one"—they honestly believed that a few plaques, cards, decals, letters, speeches, and articles would make a difference! They wanted the results without paying the price. They wanted to give lip service to the law of reciprocity without actually living the law.

Was XYZ's Values Program another example of "management by best-seller"? Unfortunately the answer is yes—but it didn't have to be. Most strategic initiatives, management development programs, and cultural change projects adopted by organizations today are philosophically sound and well intentioned. The challenge lies in getting people at all levels of the organization to admit that change does need to occur and that it must begin with them. In the case of XYZ Manufacturing, the only way to convince workers that management's intent was honorable would have been for everyone from the CEO on down to admit they had done wrong and wanted to improve. Nothing less than total candor, total commitment, and total change would have sufficed.

Eric Harvey, president of Performance Systems Corporation and a creator of both Positive Discipline Performance Management and In-Sync Management[12] systems, states, "Many managers fail to apply what they believe should be done to make things better, to their own actions. The result is that their actions are out of sync with their words. They seem surprised to learn their employees believe their actions rather than their words."

[12]Registered trademark.

Emerson put it this way: "What you are speaks so loudly I can't hear what you say." Leaders with integrity rely on their actions to send the message long before the words are ever spoken.

Having said that, let's look more closely at the Scout Law. The original words of the law are in large, bold type. The authors' commentary on the words are in lightface type.

The Scout Law

A Scout is:

> **Trustworthy.** Trust is the basis for all successful relationships. Without trust, people do not feel free to look at options for mutual success and believability diminishes. You can count on trustworthy leaders to focus on what's right rather than who's right, to be consistent in their dealings with people, and to be honest. The result is employees who will go the extra mile, customers who remain loyal, and suppliers who are willing to look for flexible ways to meet everyone's needs. Initial acceptance of an idea, product, or person is based on first impressions. Trust builds long-term support.
>
> **Loyal.** In the past, loyalty was a "given." Loyalty to employees, employers, customers, and business associates has diminished as the focus of business and life has turned toward immediate rather than long-term satisfaction. An article in the November 8, 1990, *USA Today* pointedly demonstrates how loyalty has changed. A 1925 list created by Boston University School

of Management professor Fred Foulkes cited thirty U.S. firms with "no layoff" practices. The article reported that the list had diminished to eight companies. Loyalty does not mean that a leader or an organization will never have to deal with unpleasant issues like layoffs or restructuring. The loyal leader, instead, looks for creative ways to help those they lead meet their goals. Leading with integrity requires us to be loyal to those individuals and groups on whom we depend and who depend on us.

Helpful. Zig Ziglar says, "You can get everything in life you want if you'll help enough other people get what they want." In other words, being helpful pays dividends. The dividends occur in two ways. First, you receive an internal dividend. That dividend comes in the good feeling you get when you realize that you have assisted someone in reaching a goal or solving a problem. The satisfaction alone makes helping worthwhile. Second, you receive an external dividend. It comes from the reciprocity you receive when you help others. Helping others creates an atmosphere of trust and loyalty that results in people helping you.

Friendly. Leaders may be given the right to lead, but they earn the right to be followed. Being friendly communicates a humanness that commands respect. Friendliness doesn't have to mean being best friends. It does mean acknowledging people as individuals with their own special personalities and likes.

Courteous. The root of courtesy is respect. The leader with integrity respects the opinions, beliefs, customs, and values of others. She encourages individuals to state their opinions and then listens. He respects beliefs and values and doesn't impose his own morals on others, choosing instead to let his behavior speak for him. It's easy to limit courtesy to holding the door open for others and saying please and thank you. The leader who practices courtesy does these things and more, continually looking for ways to make the people around him feel important.

Kind. Leaders who lead with integrity have high self-esteem. They have no need to make others look bad in order to make themselves look better. They demonstrate their self-esteem through kindness. Kindness is not the same as being unwilling to say something bad to someone. That trait is and is not evident in the leader we are describing. Kindness means that we design an approach that enables people to preserve their dignity and help them improve. Mary Kay Ash, founder of Mary Kay Cosmetics, puts it this way, "Whenever I have to talk with someone about a problem, I always want them to feel appreciated for who they are." Howard Putnam, former CEO of Southwest and Braniff airlines, says that he uses the practice of "getting mad at the problem, not at the person," to keep him on the right track.

Obedient. We often interpret obedience as compliance with the rules and the opposite of what it takes to succeed in today's business environment. Obedience can be positive however. The Boy Scout definition of obedient brings to mind words such as *loyal, faithful, devoted, conforming,* and *law-abiding*. The individual who leads with integrity is obedient to the rules of the organization as well as to his or her own code of honor. Obedience doesn't mean we never question or challenge the rules. But it does mean that once they are established and agreed upon, we follow them.

Cheerful. The book of Proverbs says, "a cheerful heart is good medicine." The medicine works for you and all those around you. Scientific evidence points to the fact that the individual who is cheerful experiences less stress and has better health than those who continually worry. Common sense and experience tells us that, all things being equal, people prefer to be around other people who have a cheerful outlook. For the leader in today's competitive business environment, having people who will follow is no guarantee. Being a cheerful leader can help make your organization a place where people want to work.

Thrifty. Leaders must balance progress toward a goal with the organization's survival. In business, being thrifty is the key. Long-term success depends on what you keep, not what you make. Thrifty leaders are willing to spend money, but as Roy Christenson of the Black Mountain Spring Water Company says, "We try to make their dimes work like dollars."

Brave. Historically, bravery is thought of in the physical sense. Today, bravery most often applies to the courage to follow your dreams and convictions. It is tempting to sacrifice aspirations and principles on the altar of expediency. Sticking to your goal and your principles is just as scary as physical dangers.

Clean. A former tennis coach of Randy's had a saying that describes the importance of a clean body, mind, and spirit. "If you look sharp, you feel sharp. If you feel sharp, you act sharp. If you act sharp, you play sharp. If you play sharp, you are sharp." Does appearance have a bearing on success? The answer from two perspectives is yes. First, there is the feeling of self-confidence that comes from looking and feeling your best. Most people can remember the feeling they had when they looked and felt their best. Second, the perceptions we create influence our success. Walk into a luxury store in the clothes normally reserved for painting your home and see how they treat you. Walk into the same store one week later looking your best. Were you treated differently? Hopefully not, but if we were betting people, we'd lay you two to one that you were. Appearance does make a difference. Tom Peters was right. "Perception is everything."

Reverent. Reverence is a word related to "awe." We should never lose our awe of our Creator, of creation, or of human potential.

THE SCOUT LAW IN ACTION

Have you see the Scout Law in action lately? Chances are that you have if you have heard of, or come into contact with, one of the following leaders or organizations.

Max Dupree and Herman Miller, Inc. Herman Miller is the innovative leader of the furniture industry. In 1989, it ranked ninth in *Fortune*'s listing of the one hundred best companies to work for in the United States. Herman Miller has a history of sharing the company's financial gains with all employees. While businesses everywhere were handing out golden parachutes to executives, Herman Miller was structuring silver parachutes for all employees with over two years of service.

Volvo Cars of North America. Long recognized as one of the safest cars on the road, Volvo showed its integrity with the pulling of its controversial "monster truck" ad in the fall of 1990. The ad showed a large truck running over a line of cars—and only the Volvo survived uncrushed. Later, they and everyone else discovered that the ad agency had reinforced the Volvo not because it wasn't strong enough, but simply so they could videotape it several times without replacing the vehicle. Volvo was innocent of the act, yet they not only pulled the ad, they published a letter of apology and explanation.

Ray Chambers and the One-to-One Mentoring Project. Ray Chambers made the Forbes Four Hundred List in 1986 when he was a partner in Wesray Capital Corporation. Today he is the founder of the READY program, a program that helps underprivileged youth in Newark attain an education. Chambers is now chairman of the board for One-to-One, a new partnership of business and the voluntary sector. One-to-One will serve as a national facilitator to create new partnerships among social service agencies and the private sector to effectively focus efforts to solve the problems of socially isolated and disconnected youth at community level.

The Procter & Gamble Company. P&G has a long history of commitment to quality products. Their brands include Pampers, Tide, Charmin, Bounty, Cheer, Cascade, Comet, Sure, and Scope. Most of us have used one or more P&G products. Less well known is P&G's commitment to quality benefits for their people. In 1885, when American workers expected a six-day work week, P&G began giving employees Saturday afternoon off, with pay. In 1887, they started the first profit-sharing plan in the industry. In 1915, they became one of the first companies in the country to adopt health,[13] disability, and life insurance programs for their employees.

Earlier we reported that the list of companies committed to no layoff policies dropped from thirty to eight! P&G began guaranteeing employees at least forty-eight weeks of work each year *back in 1923!* Today, P&G is pioneering by offering adoption aid benefits.

Hewlett-Packard Company. There's a good reason Hewlett-Packard is on virtually everyone's "best list." H-P has provided a model for growing a successful business and maintaining excellent employee loyalty and trust. The company maintains a highly competitive compensation and benefits package. It provides recreation areas for employees and remains committed to a tradition of full employment. The company's philosophy, articulated in "The H-P Way," stresses belief in people, respect, dignity, recognition, security, open communication, and a chance to learn and grow. The

[13]In 1915, health insurance was called "sickness insurance."

words sound good on paper—and are proven out in practice.

Delta Air Lines. Delta has long been known as one of the "best places to work" because of their family spirit. Delta maintains a practice of full employment and provides some of the best benefits in the industry. Consequently, Delta has been rewarded with excellent profits and a loyal customer base. Delta consistently rates at the top of the list in customer satisfaction.

Is Delta a *really* good place to work? Let's put it this way: When was the last time a group of *your* employees got together to give you an airplane? Delta employees raised $30 million to buy a Boeing 767 for the company as their way of saying, "Thank you for being a great place to work!"

Quad/Graphics Inc. Quad/Graphics is a company built on trust. Founded in 1920, this company invests heavily in its employees through continuous training, competitive compensations and benefits, and an environment that promotes responsibility and risk taking. At Quad/Graphics, printing is a highly regarded profession and employees are highly appreciated professionals. The results are impressive. Quad/Graphics prints for national magazines and catalogs, including the midwestern edition of *Newsweek;* advertising pages for *Time* and *U.S. News & World Report;* and regular monthly issues of *Black Enterprise.* The company has so much trust in their employees that each year they have a "Spring Fling and Management Sneak." On this day the business operates for twenty-four continuous hours— *with no managers present!*

Case Study: Ben and Jerry's Ice Cream

When best friends Ben Cohen and Jerry Greenfield decided they'd like to be in the ice-cream business, they took a five-dollar ice-cream correspondence course. Armed with all the knowledge five dollars could buy, they developed their own recipes and opened a twelve-flavor ice-cream parlor in 1978. There are now ninety stores, and sales are in excess of $58 million a year!

When entrepreneurs start small and grow to gigantic proportions, there's a great temptation to keep all the profits for themselves—after all, there's no legal law against it. Ben Cohen and Jerry Greenfield felt there was a moral law prohibiting them from "taking the money and running." From the very beginning, they became a people-oriented company. "People" includes customers, shareholders, employees, and even those who have never heard of Ben and Jerry's Ice Cream. To customers, they provide delicious, homemade-style ice cream. To shareholders, they provide a place for their investment to grow (so far earnings are reinvested instead of paid out in dividends, but the shareholders aren't complaining). To employees, they provide free ice cream, free health club memberships to work it off, inexpensive day care, and dependable employment in a family atmosphere. To the people of their communities, Ben and Jerry's provides free ice-cream for charitable fund-raisers. They set aside 7½ percent of their pretax profits to go to a nonprofit foundation.

In spite of the calorie count of their product, there are no "fat cats" at Ben and Jerry's. The health club membership is one reason. Another is that company policy dictates that no executive (including Ben and

Jerry) can earn more than five times the salary of the lowest-paid staffer! Little wonder they have no problems attracting or retaining workers! Both Ben and Jerry work full, long days and often "work the line" to see what it's like and to keep in touch with their people.

In short, Ben and Jerry, for all their success, still identify with their employees and, more important, their employees identify with them.

Tom Melohn, president of North American Tool and Die, Inc., agrees with the concept of keeping in touch with employees. He says, "If you belong to three country clubs and employ a private secretary, genuine communication with workers could be tough. Those trappings of power say one thing: 'I am better than you.'" Ben and Jerry never act better than their employees, shareholders, or customers. Therefore, they have little difficulty getting others to behave as they behave, to do as they do.

What kind of company have Ben and Jerry built? One staffed by people who are trustworthy, loyal, helpful, friendly, courteous, kind, obedient, cheerful, thrifty, brave, clean, and reverent. The kind of people who obey both legal and moral laws because they're the thing to do, not just because they're afraid of the consequences.

THE BEST TRAITS OF A LEADER

One executive we know says, "The two most important traits for any leader are truthfulness and fairness. The quality of the leader influences the quality of the product. As leaders, we must remember that employees and customers feel, 'When the CEO lies to you, the company lies to you!'"

Good images, like good buildings, take time to construct and often must be built brick by brick. Public relations can give your corporate image a boost, but you can't build an image with PR. Every employee is your image—and they depend on management to set the example. As a leader in your organization, you must serve as a role model for those above and below you on the organizational chart.

The December 4, 1989, issue of *Fortune* carried an article by Alan Farnham titled, "The Trust Gap." In this article, Farnham says, "Corporate America is split by a gulf between top management and everybody else—in pay, in perks, in self-importance." His point was that it is difficult for a line worker to feel "we're in this together" because workers rightly perceive that management has no concept of what it's like to work in the lower strata of the business.

The same article mentioned how some companies have worked to solve the problem. Hyatt Hotels sent the entire headquarters staff to work for a day changing sheets, pouring coffee, and running elevators. President Darryl Hartley-Leonard worked as a doorman for a day, alongside Bill Kurvers, full-time door captain. At first Darryl refused tips, but the other doormen soon set him straight. Farnham asks, "What did he get from his experience, besides tips?" Kurvers says, "He got respect." Darryl said, "It was the damnedest thing—employees came up to me and shook my hand. You forget how captured you are in a line job." He went on to describe the experience as a good reality check.

The same article reported that Southwest Airlines president Herb Kelleher and other officers work at least once a quarter as baggage handlers, ticket agents, and flight attendants. Kelleher said, "We're trying to create an understanding of the difficulties every person has on his job. When you're actually dealing with customers, and you're doing the job yourself, you're in a better position to appraise the effect of some new program or policy."

Native Americans used to say, "Judge no man until you have walked a mile in his moccasins." Walking with those we lead gives insight into their wants, needs, and feelings. It creates a bonding, a mutual respect that builds and grows. In the Declaration of Independence, the Founding Fathers wrote, "We hold these truths to be self-evident, that all men are created equal." If we really believe that, then we'll treat all as equals. This doesn't mean that the janitor in the building makes as much money as the president of the company, but it does mean that we treat the janitor with as much dignity.

The bottom line is that no one cares how much you know about them until they know how much you care about them. As Hyatt's Hartley-Leonard says of his experience, "Employees do feel they're living in a society of equals." How much difference does it make for employees to know that management considers them as equals? Successful organizations everywhere will tell you it makes all the difference in the world.

In the last century, Joseph De Veuster, known as Father Damien, left Belgium to devote his life to caring for the lepers on the island of Molokai, Hawaii. For many years he preached, taught, and cared for these people, but he won few converts to his religion. Then, one morning as he was dressing he noticed a leprous patch on his own skin. He began his mass that day with the words "My fellow lepers"—and for the first time, those in the leper colony began really to listen to what the priest had to say. His statue represents Hawaii in the United States Capitol in Washington, D.C.

STORIES TOO NUMEROUS TO TELL

Our research shows that there are literally hundreds of businesses and business people who actively live the Scout Law. Nearly every individual and company represented as a case study in this book is a good example, and we've sprinkled in enough bad examples to show what happens when the proper principles of honor and integrity are ignored. Robert Levering, Milton Moskowitz, and Michael Katz provide a good sampling of executives and organizations who uphold a high level of integrity in their book *The One Hundred Best Companies to Work for in America* (Addison-Wesley, 1984). *Fortune*'s annual survey of the Most Admired Companies is another good resource, as is *Inc.* magazine and *Forbes*. The key point to remember is that most successful businesses and business people use high principles to guide their daily decisions and actions. You probably won't hear about them in the media because their stories don't make the kind of scintillating copy that draws readers and viewers. Here are a few more organizations and individuals we believe deserve recognition:

Federal Express Corporation is one of a handful of U.S. companies with a practice of no layoffs. In addition, the company is well known for the quality way they treat their employees. Federal Express's attention to quality makes it the first service company to win the prestigious Malcolm Baldridge Award.

Digital Equipment Company has a practice of avoiding

layoffs. They have been successful in maintaining this practice despite intense changes and challenges in the computer industry.

Lincoln Electric has been practicing a tradition of no layoffs for more than forty years. Under the company's "guaranteed continuous employment program" workers have hours cut or are assigned to other responsibilities when jobs are slow.[14]

Armstrong Floors's operating principles set the foundation for this company. The principles promote respect, dignity, honesty, integrity, reliability, good taste, common sense, and fairness. The principles are demonstrated by excellent treatment of employees, community involvement, and quality products.

Johnson's Wax is a family-owned business that treats all employees as family. It has excellent employee benefits and like many of the organizations listed here, a practice of providing lifelong careers rather than jobs.

Cummins Engine has a reputation as a well-managed company with a social conscience. Executives are often involved in a loan program to work for charitable organizations. One former Cummins employee described his experience as one of the most rewarding of his career. People are given responsibility and challenge. Cummins was a leader in the move toward more participative management-employee relationships.

Quickie Designs was cited by *Business Ethics Magazine* as a company that helps the disabled live an active life-style. Under the direction of founder Marilyn Hamilton, a former Olympic athlete who was injured in an auto accident, the company designs and develops highly mobile wheelchairs, custom fits them, and offers

[14]"Fewer Firms Can Still Say, 'No Layoffs,'"*USA Today*, 8 November 1990.

a lifetime warranty. Quickie Designs, almost 10 percent of whose work force is disabled, has a strong commitment to improving the quality of life for its customers—because they understand the special problems their customers face.

Stoneyfield Farm is committed to agriculture, nutrition, and support of the family farm. Their yogurt received the only four-star nutrition rating among frozen desserts from the *Boston Globe*. In August 1990, *Business Ethics Magazine* recognized the company for its commitment to product integrity, quality, education, and support for the small farmer.

Patagonia is a maker of outdoor clothing that is also concerned with the outdoors. The company donates 10 percent of pretax profits to environmental causes, uses recycled paper throughout its operation, and is working to recycle 70 percent of the company's waste.

ASK Computer System doesn't just ask its employees for input—it encourages it and then acts on the information it receives. CEO Sandra Kurtzig uses employee feedback to rate managers and for reorganization of research and development.

Otis Elevator Company gives an annual community service award to eleven employees and gives a donation in their name to the organization they've volunteered to help. The company also publishes a monthly list of volunteer opportunities.

Du Pont was a pioneer in providing excellent employee benefits. Their safety record and programs are considered by many to be among the best in the industry. Du Pont is also actively involved in both national and international philanthropic projects.

Marriott Hotels are known for quality customer service, which is made possible because they've always invested in their employees. The company has a wide range of employee training and development programs and places special emphasis on hiring and training of the disabled.

South Shore Bank of Chicago was named to *Business Ethics* Hall of Fame in 1990 "for demonstrating that a traditional, for-profit bank can be a power engine of community revitalization." The bank has channeled money into an impoverished area, promoted local business ownership, and been involved in counseling, education, and employment programs. The outcome is the extraordinary comeback of a neighborhood many had written off—*and a $1.4 million profit for the bank in 1989!*

The Sandy River Group builds long-term health-care facilities for the elderly. Each facility is designed and built to accommodate the needs of its residents. The company's actions are taken because the firm has a philosophy that business has an obligation to society that extends beyond profits.

Black Mountain Spring Water Company believes that its integrity is demonstrated by its service. To make sure that integrity is maintained, the company limited its geographic growth in 1989. According to Roy Christensen, vice president of marketing and operations, and Steve Block, vice president of sales, "To provide the kind of service we promised our customers, we had no other choice. A company of integrity can never promise more than they can produce."

H. B. Fuller has adopted some of the chemical industries' highest environmental standards. Their goal is *no pollution* of the air, ground, or water. President and CEO Anthony Anderson says, "It's tough to look at a budget and see the dollars for a scrubber or water-cleansing system. But we look beyond that cost to the long-range cost of not doing it."

Perrier Group of America voluntarily pulled its products from the shelves in 1990 because a trace of benzine gas was found in some of its bottled water. The trace was the result of an unchanged filter. Perrier responded with a total recall that could have been suicide for a company that depends on its products being available to consumers, though the FDA found no danger to the public and did not ask for the action. By taking a course of action that was morally straight, Perrier willingly sacrificed short-term profits for long-term return. They decided to be leaders with integrity and stay true to their values of honesty and quality, realizing that no public relations campaign can restore consumer trust once it is lost.

Wal-Mart became the number two U.S. retailer in 1990 and could move into the number one slot by the end of 1991. Wal-Mart's growth has been phenomenal since the first store opened in 1962. Many reasons have been given for their success, but we believe founder Sam Walton's integrity is at the top of the list. Walton spends time with his associates (Wal-Mart's term for employees), is approachable, friendly, respectful, and courteous with all. Wal-Mart's corporate goal is to cut costs and pass the savings on to their customers—a goal that also applies to their Spartan corporate offices. Wal-Mart associates have no trouble understanding the company's commitment to friendly, cost-efficient service—because they see it in their own management.

H. J. Heinz Company cares about its products and the people who make them. Henry J. Heinz supported the 1906 move for a pure food and drug law in Congress—a law opposed by many food industry leaders. Today, Heinz is still known for quality food products. In addition, the company is known for fostering a family atmosphere in their operation via open communication and employee recognition. H. J. Heinz is also involved in numerous philanthropic activities, including funding of infant nutrition studies in China and Thailand.

Samsonite Corporation was founded in 1910 by Jesse Shwayder with his life savings—$3,500—and a firm conviction that the Golden Rule was the only way to do business. Jesse felt that the quality he'd want in his own luggage was strength—luggage as strong as Samson in the Bible. Samson was the first name of Shwayder products, and it later became Samsonite—a brand known and recognized for quality around the world. Through all the years, however, adherence to the Golden Rule never varied. Each new employee is given a Golden Rule marble (Samsonite provides the marbles that Mary Kay Ash and "Foots" Clements give away) to remind them of the company's philosophy. Samsonite has pioneered many firsts in luggage—first vinyl, first to promote fashion colors, first to use ABS plastic and magnesium, first to use hidden locks—yet the basic principle of following the Golden Rule in relations with customers, suppliers, and employees has never changed.

Arthur Andersen & Company, one of the nation's largest accounting and consulting firms, is addressing the issue of business ethics and integrity by funding a five-year, five-million-dollar program to help bring the subject into the business school curriculum. Participating colleges and universities are provided with free conferences for faculty, videotapes, and case studies to assist them in better preparing students for the dilemmas waiting in the "real world."

The Scout Law—How to Know It When You See It

We've shared a number of examples of the Scout Law in action, but our list is neither definitive nor exhaustive. You probably know others, many right in your own community. You can identify them by answering the following questions.

• What businesses and business people come to mind when you think of trust?

Business/business
leaders you trust   Why do you trust them?

_____   _____

_____   _____

_____   _____

_____   _____

_____   _____

_____   _____

_____   _____

• When you think "Best Customer Service" you have encountered, what name(s) come to mind?

Names   Why do you rate them so highly?

_____   _____

_____   _____

_____   _____

_____   _____

_____   _____

_____   _____

_____   _____

• When you think of quality products, what name(s) come to mind?

Names   Why do you rate them so highly?

_____   _____
_____   _____
_____   _____
_____   _____
_____   _____
_____   _____
_____   _____

Chances are that the individuals and organizations you listed have the habit of living the Scout Law. As we said earlier in this chapter, most companies that are successful over the long run have made these principles part of their "corporate culture." We have seen in the case studies that the leader sets the example for the organization's behavior. *Did your organization make the list?* Why or why not? If not, there are probably some things you can learn from your own responses that will help you honor your commitment to obeying the Scout Law.

"ON MY HONOR, I WILL"

Things I will do to honor my commitment to keep the Scout Law:

• _____
_____
_____

- _____
  _____
  _____
  _____

- _____
  _____
  _____
  _____

- _____
  _____
  _____
  _____

- _____
  _____
  _____
  _____

CHAPTER SEVEN

On my honor, I will do my best:
1. To do my duty to God and my country, and to obey
the Scout Law;

TO HELP OTHER PEOPLE
AT ALL TIMES

Almost anyone will help other people *some*times—a Scout pledges to help other people at *all times*. As leaders with integrity, this must be our goal as well. We discussed the importance of laws that yield predictable results in the previous chapter. The law of reciprocity applies to everything you do. If you help other people at all times, then you'll find people willing to help you too. "Giving to get" should not be your motivation, but "give and it shall be given to you" is a principle that transcends borders.

Who are these "other people" you should be helping at all times? From a business perspective, there are three groups: customers, employees, and community. Like other principles in this book, the concept of helping others at all times applies in our personal lives as well. Highest on your priority list should be those you love, followed by those you like, those you work with and for, those in your community, your country, and the world at large.

As we mentioned earlier, our destinies and our futures are inextricably intertwined. For a very simple reason, those in the stern cannot refuse to help if they hear water is pouring into the bow, though the bow is far away: If the bow sinks, the stern follows. We not only share common disaster but also common good.

It is one thing to decide to help others, but *how* do we help them? The main thing to remember about help is that genuine help means giving them what *they* want and need—not necessarily what *we want and need*. True help means assisting them in obtaining their goals—not enlisting their aid in helping us obtain our own.

What would you think if a pesky neighbor rang your doorbell at six in the morning on Saturday and announced, "I've come over to help you paint your house orange!" You'd probably reply, "I don't want to paint my house, and if I did, I certainly wouldn't paint it orange." Suppose he got angry and shouted, "Your house needs painting and I got the orange paint on sale! What's the matter with you, don't you want your house to look nice? Boy, some people just don't appreciate someone who tries to help!"

We behave just as foolishly when we try to help anyone obtain what we want them to have instead of what they want. To be a real help, in the Boy Scout tradition, we must find what they want and need and assist them in meeting their goals.

How do you find out what people want and need? The answer is surprisingly simple: You ask them.

Peter Megargee Brown, in his book *The Art of Ques-*

tioning, says, "At the start of World War II the story went around that the United States Army spent millions of dollars researching which soldiers should be sent to warm climates of the South Pacific and which should be sent to the cold northern climates of Europe. . . . Army officials finally came to the conclusion . . . simply to ask the soldiers this question: 'Do you like warm weather or cold weather?' The problem was solved." The same approach works when leaders want to know the needs of their customers, employers, and communities—just ask.

HELPING CUSTOMERS AT ALL TIMES

Ralph Waldo Emerson observed, "Society is always taken by surprise at any new example of common sense." Our fascination with quality and customer service are but two of the latest examples. Integrity as a basis for leading is a third.

It's not surprising that successful leaders and organizations help their customers get what they want and need at all times. What is surprising is that more leaders haven't figured out that integrity in your customer relationships is the key to success. Michael LeBoeuf, Ph.D., cites the following statistics in his book *How to Win Customers and Keep Them for Life:*[15]

- *A typical business hears from only 4 percent of its dissatisfied customers. The other 96 percent go quietly away and 91 percent will never come back.*
- *In a survey of why customers quit, 68 percent quit because of an attitude of indifference toward the customer by the owner, manager, or some employee.*

[15]Berkley, 1987.

- *Businesses having low service quality average only a 1 percent return on sales and lose market share at the rate of 2 percent per year. Businesses with high service quality average a 12 percent return on sales, gain market share at the rate of 6 percent a year, and charge significantly higher prices.*

It is the customer who pays the bills, finances the growth, and makes it possible to stay in business. Creating and keeping customers is every employee's most important priority. Helping customers at all times then is the lifeblood of any organization.

What does it mean to help customers at all times? It means giving them what they want, the way they want it, at the time they want it, at a price they are willing to pay. Whether your customers are internal or external, your success depends on helping them at all times.

People make buying decisions for a wide variety of reasons—product quality, service, convenience, usefulness, status, value, etc. The days of offering one basic product with one basic service plan are gone forever. Henry Ford was able to joke you could buy one of his cars "in any color you want as long at it's black," but that attitude didn't last long. Today's customers expect more for their money. They expect value and honest information about the products and services you provide. They expect your products and services to be exactly what you promised, and they want them at their own convenience—not yours.

Michael LeBoeuf identifies five qualities a company should be to keep customers coming back:

Reliable
Credible
Attractive
Responsive
Empathic.

Most organizations operate this way during start-up. They are hungry for customers and treat each one with dignity and respect. Unfortunately, as the business grows it becomes more and more difficult to maintain that initial level of customer service. At this point, small organizations sometimes lose some customers because they just don't have the staff or systems to maintain the quality of service their customers expect. In larger organizations, complacency often creeps in as employees decide *that much service* really isn't necessary and management decides it's okay to lose a few customers, since there are plenty of others who do business with the firm. Large or small, any business that decides customers are expendable is doomed.

As a case in point, several employees at a client company that filed Chapter 11 reported that they were happy when there weren't a lot of customers! They and their peers had often complained about being *too busy!* Service deteriorated. Revenues dropped, and by the time they realized the effects of their behavior, it was too late. Their customers had abandoned them, and they were unable to secure new ones. (Do you think the former employees are happy there are no customers today?)

When one of the authors of this book was arranging a large party at a restaurant, the owner attempted to change both the agreed-upon price and the menu— claiming the author's wife had agreed to it. When the author was unsuccessful at obtaining the original menu, he reluctantly said he would have to cancel because his wife would never be happy with the menu as it was now presented. The author realized any possibility of successful negotiations was over when the owner said, "I'm not in business just to satisfy people and make people happy. I'm in business to make money!" The author hopes that by now the restaurant owner has realized that any organization that's not in business to satisfy customers and make them happy *cannot possibly stay in business!*

Here are a few points to remember as you work to help satisfy your customers and make them happy!

- *Perception is reality.* If customers say you aren't meeting their needs, then you aren't meeting their needs. Period.
- *Little things mean a lot.* You demonstrate your commitment to helping the customer by the little things that you do. Paying attention to the details sends a message of integrity and concern. As one executive says, "Take care of the little things and the big things often take care of themselves."
- *Complaints are good news.* This sounds strange, but people and organizations learn from customer feedback. If someone will take the time to let you know how they feel, it is important enough for you to listen to their opinion. Ken Blanchard and Spencer Johnson, writing in *The One Minute Manager,*[16] make the statement, "Feedback is the breakfast of champions." Good organizations want to hear what their customers have to say.
- *Great service doesn't take the place of quality products*; you must have both. There are people and organizations who assume that a smile and an apology will make up for lack of quality—it won't. A smile and an apology

[16] William Morrow and Company, 1982.

will work once, but the quality must be there if you
want them to keep coming back.

- *There are two components to quality products and services.*
  The first component is doing it right the first time.
  The second is having systems in place to catch and
  correct mistakes when they do occur.
- *Everyone likes to feel good about themselves.* They want to
  feel they made the right decision, that they are important, that they are valuable. People like to do business
  and associate with people who make them feel important.

Employees must carry the message that the organization wants to help customers at all times. Leaders and
organizations of integrity understand the relationship
between helping employees and helping customers,
and they actively work to make the employee/customer
connection a positive one. J. W. "Bill" Marriott, chairman and president of the Marriott Corporation, emphasizes the employee connection with these words:
"Motivate them, train them, care about them, and
make winners out of them.... We know that if we treat
our employees correctly, they'll treat the customers
right. And if customers are treated right, they'll come
back."[17] Since taking care of your employees is so
important to taking care of your customers, let's take a
look at how you can help them!

HELPING EMPLOYEES AT ALL TIMES

Ask a typical executive what their employees want from
a job, the response will be "money." If they have a

[17]"Ten Million Chances to Excel," *Empowering Business Resources*, Scott, Foresman
and Company, 1990.

moment to think about it, they often add "security."
Money and security are important, but they aren't all
today's workers want from a job. The *most important*
thing they want is job satisfaction. Job satisfaction includes pay and security, but also includes opportunity,
fulfillment, encouragement, coaching, a sense of partnership, respect, and integrity. Helping them means
you provide skills, support, opportunity, and role models to assist them in obtaining satisfaction in their jobs.
When it comes to pay, employees also want their compensation to be based on the work they do and the
importance of that work—not just by job title or classi-
fication. Management consultant Steve Ventura uses
the following exercise to drive home the importance of
money for job satisfaction:

> Think of your favorite job of all times, the one
> you would choose if you could have any job
> you wanted. Write that job in the space below:
>
> _____
>
> Would you do that job for:
> 1% less than you make today?   ___ yes ___ no
> 5% less than you make today?   ___ yes ___ no
> 10% less than you make today?   ___ yes ___ no
> 25% less than you make today?   ___ yes ___ no

Most people respond that they would do their "favorite"
job for 1 percent less than they make today. Almost no
one says yes to a 25 percent decrease. Somewhere
between 1 and 25 percent, life-style, obligations, financial goals, and values took over and influenced the
response. The point is, that if you answered yes to
doing a job for 1 percent less than you make today, you

have said other things are as, or more, important to you than money. In the spaces below, list the job factors that you consider part of your "ideal job."

- _____
- _____
- _____
- _____
- _____
- _____
- _____
- _____

If you found these factors to be important in your ideal job, do you think others will too? So do we!

Ask children what they want to be when they grow up and watch them play make-believe. They'll tell you they want to be doctors, cowboys, cowgirls, ball players, pilots, firefighters, etc. The common factor is that the vocations they aspire to make them feel important because they are exciting, fun, glamorous, or important. No one ever pretends to be someone who is bored, angry, and unappreciated.

Children get excited about their "ideal jobs." Adults do too! There are many employees in every organization hoping for that "ideal job." It's so prevalent that management programs exist to create those kinds of jobs. Participative management, quality circles, and self-managed work teams are all great tools to help give employees what they want. Unfortunately, many of these programs achieve less than satisfactory results.

Judith Vogt and Bradley Hunt, writing in the May 1988 *Training and Development Journal*, suggest that 50 percent of current participative work groups will dissolve. We believe that the root cause of the failure is a lack of trust—which is another way of saying that the work groups doubt the integrity of management. Before you can help employees create their ideal job, they have to trust your motives and intentions.

HOW TO KNOW IF THERE IS A PERCEIVED LACK OF INTEGRITY

There are many excellent tools available to determine employee perceptions. Unfortunately, most of these tools are applicable only to large organizations. Whether your organization is large or small, here are some simple ways to "check the pulse." You'll know there's a potential challenge when you find:

• Decreased support for the organization's mission and vision.
• Increased turnover.
• Increased absenteeism not related to specific illness.
• Increased number of disputes, complaints, or grievances.
• Questioning of management support for new initiatives or changes.
• Increased reliance on outside or formal sources to resolve issues of "unfair treatment."

When employees repeatedly question your motives or intentions, it's usually because they got burned in the past. Maybe not by you, but burned nevertheless. We all carry the baggage of experience into each new situation. If that experience was bad, our baggage is often filled with mistrust.

HOW TO GET INTEGRITY BACK ON TRACK

The fact you want to build or regain credibility and are committed to leading with integrity is a good start to getting integrity in your workplace back on track. The people you lead will soon know whether or not you're sincere. Your commitment will be proven, over time, by your actions. Here are some ideas to get integrity back on track where you work:

- *Ask employees for their perceptions.* If they don't trust you, they may not be honest with you, so provide a way for them to give you anonymous feedback.
- *Acknowledge their perceptions.* Feelings are neither right nor wrong—they're just feelings. You may disagree with what they say, but don't be defensive. You are all working toward a common goal—a better relationship.
- *Acknowledge your shortcomings.* Admit it when you have acted inappropriately. We all have a great capacity for forgiveness when someone confesses a fault freely.
- *Realize the process takes time.* Problems take time to develop, solutions take time to implement, perceptions take time to change.
- *Continually ask for feedback.* Periodically, ask people how you're doing and listen to their comments. Your willingness to ask and listen sends a message that you understand the importance of credibility, trust, and integrity.
- *Treat people with dignity and respect at all times.* Educator Booker T. Washington, writer of the classic book *Up from Slavery* and founder of the Tuskegee Institute,

said, "There can be no real social progress in this country until we realize there is as much dignity in tilling a field as there is in writing a poem." Not as much *money*—as much *dignity*. The janitor is not entitled to as much money as the president, but he or she is entitled to as much dignity.

CAN HELPING OTHERS BACKFIRE?

A comedian once lamented, "No good deed goes unpunished." Sometimes, even when we do the right thing for the right reasons, it doesn't turn out as we might have wished. A leader may invest a lot of time and talent in helping and developing a subordinate, then the subordinate will leave. This should not discourage you. People who are going to leave are going to leave regardless. Your efforts to help people be all they can be mean their association with you was more valuable while they were there. Your personal interest may have enabled them to find opportunities in your organization for a longer time and thus have prolonged their stay. (Besides, there is something worse than spending the time and money to train a person and having them leave, *and that is not training them and having them stay!*)

Case Study: Mary Kay Ash

Mary Kay Ash founded Mary Kay Cosmetics in 1963, and since that time, it has grown to more than 200,000 employees and beauty consultants in twelve countries with wholesale sales of more than $450 million a year! How did it begin? Mary Kay says,

I had opinions about the organizations I'd worked for. There had been many things I thought should have been done another way.... I decided to write my memoirs—actually, a book that would help other women overcome some of the obstacles I had encountered. First, I wrote down all the good things the companies I had been with had done and then the changes I would make to create a company that was based on the Golden Rule. Wouldn't it be marvelous, I kept thinking, if someone would actually start such a company? And then I realized that I didn't have to sit and wish—I could start that dream company because I had already discovered the ideal product.... To me, 'P and L' meant more than *profit* and *loss*—it meant *people* and *love*.

People and love are descriptive words for Mary Kay Cosmetics. Mary Kay Ash doesn't just talk about loving people—she lives it. That's what has made her one of the most respected business people in America. The love begins with her sales force and employees and extends to customers.

Mary Kay Ash believes that you must lead with integrity, whether you're leading an organization or a work unit. Integrity means you put God first, family second, and career third. Management believes they must "walk their talk" in order to get the message across. While the company doesn't force religion on anyone, Mary Kay says that by setting the example, people come to their own conclusion that her philosophy is for real.

Not many companies would blatantly say that they want you to place your family above your career. Those that do are often strapped for examples of how they put that into action—not so at Mary Kay Cosmetics. At Mary Kay Cosmetics, the proof is in the performance. Company employees are told anytime there's a family need, all they have to do to be excused from work is notify their manager. Family is so important to the company that each year they invite employees and their families to the Six Flags over Texas amusement park for their company picnic—and pick up all the expenses. They give turkeys to all employees the Monday before Thanksgiving (so the birds have time to properly thaw) and share the cost of annual mammograms for female employees.

In addition to promoting strong family values, they also try to maintain a family atmosphere at work. It's an informal company, and there are no titles on any of the office doors.

Everyone knows that top salespeople at Mary Kay get a pink Cadillac. But the company does a great job of training and encouraging at all levels to get them to that Cadillac. No matter how many mistakes are made, they focus the trainee on what went *right*—not what went *wrong*. Each consultant receives a ribbon for her first $100 show, another for her first $200 show, and so on. Milestones are marked with diamond rings and trips abroad. At awards ceremonies, as many people as possible are publicly rewarded and praised. They honor initial and entry-level achievements all the way up to the crowning of the queen, complete with satin sashes, tiaras, bouquets of long-stemmed roses (pink, of course), and prizes like diamond rings, mink coats, and the crown jewel—diamond bumblebees. Why a bumblebee? Because of its weight and wing configuration it is aerodynamically impossible for the bumblebee to fly— but the bumblebee doesn't know it and *flies anyway!*

With this much enthusiasm, some are initially skeptical. Many people find it hard to believe that Mary Kay Cosmetics is for real—but it is. In a world filled with hyperbole and sales hype, it's easy to become somewhat jaundiced about a company's claims to care. Executives at Mary Kay know that, and they are patient, believing that integrity will eventually win the skeptical over. Mary Kay herself puts it simply: "When you walk your talk, people know it and respond positively."

Mary Kay considers customers part of the family too. They offer a money-back guarantee on all merchandise sold—even if the container is empty when it's returned. They have a staff of medically trained professionals and a lab to answer customer questions about any adverse reactions to products.

Mary Kay Ash leads with integrity for two reasons:

- She knows that's the way she wants to be treated.
- She knows that helping employees, salespeople and customers at all times is good business.

Satisfying the needs of others is what leading with integrity is all about. If you don't look out for others, then you can't run a happy or proud organization. If you help other people, do it honestly and with integrity. Take care of others and they will take care of you.

Case Study: Carl Sewell, Sewell Village Cadillac

Carl Sewell's automobile dealerships not only sell Cadillac, but Lexus, Oldsmobile, and Hyundai cars. He has built his company into one of the top car dealerships in America. He didn't start that way, but he reached his goal by continually applying one simple principle—

turning "one-time" buyers into lifetime customers. In the endorsement for Sewell's book, *Customers for Life*,[18] Stew Leonard says, "So often when we read business books, two things cross our minds: (1) 'I wonder if the author follows his own teachings?' and (2) 'If the author is so smart, why isn't he rich?' Well, in Carl Sewell's case, the $250 million business he built answers both questions."

How does Sewell build customers for life? For the details, we recommend that you read his book, but in general, he continually helps employees and customers. Examples abound:

- free loan cars
- extended service hours (Saturdays and evenings)
- personal contact with customers
- attention to detail (grounds, cars, rest rooms)
- incentives and rewards for employees that help turn prospects into customers for life.

Here is one customer's perception about Sewell's operation:

"My wife and I knew we wanted to go in and check out the cars and deals at Sewell. I had heard about their tradition of product and service quality in one of Tom Peters's books and in *Inc.* magazine. We were impressed by the appearance of the building, and by the recommendations of other Sewell customers.

We knew we had made a good decision as soon as we walked through the door. The showroom was spacious, comfortable, and ele-

[18]Doubleday/Currency, 1990.

gant. The receptionist smiled and welcomed us, and the salesperson let us know he was there to help without being a nuisance. We made a decision to do business with Sewell based on the service we received before the sale. We'll continue because of the service we've received after the sale. The service staff is friendly, efficient, and provides professional service. Our salesperson continues to follow up periodically to make sure certain things are going well. As customers, we have the protection of free service calls for emergencies. To top it off, we received a personal invitation to a party just for Sewell customers to view the new year models—and entertainment was provided by the Glen Miller Orchestra!"

Obviously, Sewell does a lot of things right from the customer's perspective. One of the most important things they do to take good care of their customers is to take good care of their employees! They provide good compensation and continual training for all their employees, which enables them to attain and retain exceptional people. The salesperson who worked with this customer left an executive position in the financial services industry to sell automobiles.

Is the experience just quoted a common one at Sewell? J. D. Powers and Associates found Sewell Village Cadillac's customer service scores were 31.5 percent higher than the national average! There are a lot of reasons for this high level of customer satisfaction— but the bottom line is integrity!

In *Customers for Life*, Sewell gives his views on integrity. "People spend an awful lot of time watching what the boss does. And if the boss wants his employees to act ethically, he'd better behave that way himself.... We tell our people they should always ask themselves, 'How would my actions appear if they were described tomorrow on the front page of the local newspaper?'"

It's obvious that Carl Sewell believes his words. It is also obvious that his employees and customers do too!

HELPING COMMUNITIES AT ALL TIMES

Helping people at all times means *getting involved*. It is caring, and sharing, and service in action. A whole nation was ashamed when a woman was raped in broad daylight on a public sidewalk and other pedestrians merely stopped to watch. We are not a nation of cowards, but even if everyone in the crowd lacked the physical or moral courage to come to the woman's aid, couldn't someone have at least summoned aid? If we reap what we sow, what happens when we ignore crime in the streets, hopelessness, illiteracy, environmental hazards, or political corruption because we don't want to "get involved"? Unfortunately, we are finding out!

Martin Neimoller, a Lutheran pastor in Nazi Germany in the 1930s, summed up eloquently the final result of not getting involved. "In Germany, they came first for the Communists, and I didn't speak up because I wasn't a Communist. Then they came for the Jews, and I didn't speak up because I wasn't a Jew. Then they came for the trade unionists, and I didn't speak up because I wasn't a trade unionist. Then they came for the Catholics, and I didn't speak up because I was a Protestant. Then they came for me, and by that time, no one was left to speak up." Neimoller lived to know the full import of the words Edmund Burke wrote a hundred and fifty years earlier, "The only thing necessary for the triumph of evil is for enough good men to do nothing."

The most quoted excuse for not getting involved is "It's not my job." Business people step over the homeless in their path because helping them is "not my job." Charitable organizations are unable to provide resources because those asked to give say, "It's not my job." At times, this excuse can go to ridiculous lengths. Peter Brown tells of a patron in Lindy's restaurant on Broadway in New York who asked a passing waiter, "Can you tell me what time it is?" The waiter replied, "Sorry, sir, but that's not my table!" Giving someone else's customer the time of day was "not my job."

Leaders with integrity don't worry about whose job it is—they get involved. They feel that helping others "is their job"—and they teach others to feel the same way. When Robert Haas took over Levi Strauss and Company in 1984, he called his executives together and told them he would require them to disclose how they had contributed to the success of others at salary and performance reviews. Haas wanted to know what each executive had done to ensure the company's success—but he felt their contributions to the success of others within the organization and the community were just as important. Today, leaders everywhere are encouraging contribution to the community. And they are providing positive role models for those they lead.

It's easy to ask a spouse, a family member, a coworker, or an employee what kind of help they need. How do you ask your community or your country? The answer is there are so many needs it is beyond the resources and capabilities of any one person to help meet them all. Pick the areas that seem most vital to you, then contact those in charge of those areas and ask, "How can I help you?" Once they have recovered from their faint, they'll tell you!

Helping others at all times means we not only listen to what the communities *want* but also help them determine what they *need*. And if we have to make a decision, we choose to *help meet the need rather than the want*. As Booker T. Washington said, "If you give a man a fish, you give him a meal. If you teach him how to fish, he can feed himself—and someone else too." True helping is encouraging and empowering others to be all they can be. After all, a best friend is someone who brings out the best in you—not someone who tells you things are fine when they aren't but someone who tells you what's wrong and helps you make it right. A best friend is someone who encourages you to do your best to fix the problem. The leaders who lead with integrity give back to their community in ways that not only meet immediate needs but also foster solutions.

If everyone tried to help others at all times, there would be no problems with hazardous waste, abandoned neighborhoods, gangs, and illiteracy. There would be no homeless problem, and very little need for a welfare system. There would have been no need for President Bush's "thousand points of light" speech—or for this book—or for a Boy Scout Oath. Helping other people at all times is to "love your neighbor as yourself" in action.

Case Study: Dr. Stanley Pearle and Pearle, Inc.

Dr. Stanley Pearle founded Pearle Vision in 1961 with the opening of the first store in Savannah, Georgia. Today, Pearle, Inc., is part of Grand Metropolitan and is the largest retail optical company in the world, with over one thousand stores in the United States, Puerto Rico, Canada, Taiwan, Japan, the Netherlands, and Belgium. Dr. Pearle serves as a consultant to the company and participates in the meeting of the Pearle Executive Committee. He says, "We began with the philosophy that the public would respond favorably to conveniently located, attractive optical centers that offered a combination of quality products, a large selection of styles, reasonable prices, and most important, a staff of competent personnel that could provide excellent professional services." Dr. Pearle is fond of saying, "The customer is smarter than you think. You must deliver what you promise. That is the only way to develop trust."

The concept of integrity at Pearle extends throughout the organization. The company's leadership style emphasizes fair compensation, promotions based on merit, responsibility, candidness, and truthfulness. Most promotions are made from within the company. Dr. Pearle often cites the example of Del McNally, who began as a stock clerk in 1966 and rose to become a vice president of merchandising and the largest purchaser of eyewear frames in the world.

Dr. Pearle believes that management has an obligation to give something back to the community in addition to helping the company grow. He has been active in community affairs and served as president of both the Dallas United Way and Jewish Foundation. He gives a lot of credit in the building of his character to his experiences first as a Boy Scout and later as an assistant Scoutmaster. About community service he says, "You shouldn't brag about your community service or people will doubt your integrity. Also, you shouldn't do community service for business gain, but simply because it's the right thing to do."

Howard Stanworth, president and CEO of Pearle, Inc., agrees. He says, "All citizens, individual or corporate, have a responsibility for the social health of the community, as well as their own financial well-being. Commerce should provide constructive community support from the inside and understand the issues that preserve good quality of life for the members of that community, whether those issues relate to the environment, employment, security, or education."

Does the company practice what it preaches? Indeed it does. In 1987, the company created the Pearle Vision Foundation dedicated to the preservation and optimization of lifetime vision. It delivers direct benefits to hardship cases requiring urgent care. The foundation has provided treatment for cataracts, eye muscle disorders, and sight-threatening accidents, as well as eye exams and eyeglasses for disadvantaged families.

Grand Metropolitan, Pearle, Inc.'s, parent company, also has a long tradition of community involvement. Sir Allen Sheppard, chairman and group chief executive, clearly stated the organization's position in the following statement:

> At Grand Metropolitan, we measure performance by profitability and return on investment, but there is another significant measure—how we fulfill our responsibility to the communities from which our profits are derived.... It is not just sound business sense for us to care about the environment and communities within which we work and live, it is common sense to contribute to the quality of life in our communities.

The corporate philosophy at Grand Metropolitan is summed up in a simple phrase: "We aim to help people in need help themselves."

There are hundreds of good examples to follow, and many have already been mentioned in previous chapters. A few other quick examples are:

- **Jerry Junkins, president of Texas Instruments**, who has led TI to become one of the nation's leading corporations in assisting education—especially among the disadvantaged.
- **I.B.M.**, whose "executives on campus" program sends their top performers to the classroom to teach college students what they've learned "in the real world."
- **David Kerns, retired CEO at Xerox**, who heads up One-to-One, a partnership of the business and volunteer sector that provides mentoring to "at risk" youth in this country.
- **Apple Computer**, which has donated computers to schools to train the leaders of tomorrow.
- **Harold S. Hook, chairman and CEO of American General Corporation**, who has led his company to become the fourth largest shareholder-owned insurance group in the United States, is an active Boy Scout volunteer. He has worked in positions from local troop leader to president of the Boy Scouts National Board, where he focuses his energy on developing local Scoutmasters.
- **Du Pont** has turned its Wilmington, Delaware, office complex into a wildlife habitat.
- **Dayton Hudson Corporation**, parent company of Hudsons, Daytons, Target, Marshall Fields, and Mervyns retail stores, gives 5 percent of their taxable profits directly to services that benefit the communities in

which they operate. Contributions in 1990 exceeded $30 million.

These leaders are among the "thousand points of light" that President Bush talked about in his acceptance speech in 1988. They are letting the light of their experience, their knowledge, and their caring shine out among others. What do they get out of it? Primarily the satisfaction of having done a good deed—and the knowledge that "what goes around, comes around." They know that by helping others they ensure their own success.

There is an old parable about a visitor who was shown two banquet halls filled with people. In the first hall, no one was eating. When the visitor asked why, he was told that the king had tied a long spoon to each guest's arm so that they couldn't bend their elbows. Therefore, though the table was loaded with food, no one was able to convey it to their mouth! In the next room, everyone was eating and having a wonderful time. Oh, these guests also had the long spoons tied to their arms—*but each guest fed someone else!* By helping others, we are helping ourselves.

When Ronald Reagan was president of the United States he had a sign on his desk that read, "There is no limit to what you can accomplish if you don't care who gets the credit." By the same token, there is no limit to what you can accomplish in helping others if you don't care who gets the credit. If you're doing it so others will think you're a great man or woman, that's good. But if you're doing it so that the recipient of your help thinks they did it all themselves, that's even better.

Below is a questionnaire to help you evaluate what kind of job you're currently doing to help other people at all times. Afterward, there's a commitment sheet to help you focus on how you can do more.

Helping Other People Questionnaire

In what activities are you currently involved for the purpose of helping other people?

_____

_____

_____

_____

What is the scope of your involvement? (Time, money, organizational resources, etc.)

_____

_____

_____

_____

What do you expect in return for your involvement in these activities?

_____

_____

_____

_____

What have you received from your involvement in these activities?

_____

_____

_____

_____

In an earlier chapter, we quoted John Donne's admonition to remember that all of mankind is tied together in life and death. We are not only diminished by death, but by inefficiencies, insecurities, lack of knowledge, lack of resources, and lack of opportunities. The Boy Scouts knew in 1907 that helping others is a mandate for success, character, and integrity. Generations before and since have realized the same thing. We hope you will realize it too.

"ON MY HONOR, I WILL"

Things I will do to help other people at all times.

- _____
  _____
  _____
- _____
  _____
  _____
- _____
  _____
  _____
- _____
  _____
  _____
- _____
  _____
  _____

CHAPTER EIGHT

On my honor, I will do my best:
1. To do my duty to God and my country, and to obey the Scout Law;
2. To help other people at all times;

TO KEEP MYSELF PHYSICALLY STRONG, MENTALLY AWAKE, AND MORALLY STRAIGHT

The founding fathers of Scouting knew that survival and success in a challenging, and often hostile, world would depend on their recruits' abilities to effectively respond to any situation. The pledge to keep oneself physically strong, mentally awake, and morally straight recognizes the role of body, mind, and spirit in creating a healthy individual, prepared to meet the challenges and opportunities that arise. Although the world has changed since Scouting's inception, the importance of being personally prepared to survive and succeed in an often hostile world has not diminished.

Thanks to the work of people such as Bernie Siegel and Carl and Stephanie Simonton, many have learned specific techniques to control their own health. The

Simontons and James L. Creighton state in their book *Getting Well Again*,[19] "Everyone participates in his/her health or illness at all times." The foundations of holistic medicine stand on the three-legged stool of body, mind, and spirit. It is only by mastering all three that we can lead a truly healthy life.

A Scout's promise to remain physically strong, mentally awake, and morally straight uses the same components to ensure preparation for success in honoring commitments and providing leadership. Being physically strong and mentally awake prepares the Scout to meet and deal with challenges as they arise. Being morally straight guides the Scout's actions to ensure their consistency with accepted values. All three work together to ensure success.

TO KEEP MYSELF PHYSICALLY STRONG

Today, few Americans earn their living through sheer physical strength. Most of the strenuous physical labor once done by men and women is done by machines, or machines assist us in doing it. This has not changed the necessity to remain physically strong. In fact, the increased use of machines means we must take even more responsibility for our own health and vitality. The Simontons and James L. Creighton report that the rise in heart disease and cancer parallels the rise of affluent, sedentary life-styles that accompanied increased industrialization. One reason for the decrease in our physical strength is that we are eating more and eating the wrong things while doing less—a situation easily remedied.

[19]Bantam Books, 1980.

A second reason for the decreased state of our health is increased stress. People often laugh when a friend longs for the simpler life of the "good old days." But it's true that life was simpler a couple of generations back. Today, we live in a stressful world, and stress affects us not only mentally but physically as well. As long ago as the 1920s, Hans Selye at the University of Prague found a strong connection between stress and physical strength. He noted that stress can affect bodily functions, cause hormonal imbalances, lead to damaged arteries, and result in immune system malfunctions.

Our early ancestors had a way of dealing with stress: immediately following a stressful situation, they reacted physically by fight or flight. This was true whether the stress came from a mastodon attack or an arrow in the shoulder. Many of the situations in which we find ourselves today do not offer the opportunity for physical release. Without that release, the body builds up stress, affecting our ability to perform at our best and possibly causing physical problems as well. If stress is a part of your life, there are several good books on the subject that can either help eliminate the stress or control your reaction to it.

Becoming physically strong is primarily a matter of becoming physically fit. Physical fitness, according to George Sheehan III, M.D., makes a person feel at home in the environment and enables him to make responses or perform acts. It also counterbalances the results of a sedentary life-style.

There are a number of good books and programs available for becoming physically fit. We suggest you consult your physician about your individual needs. If you haven't engaged in physical activity for a while, doing too much too soon can be dangerous. As a rule of thumb, however, we like the principles of fitness Sheehan provided in an essay entitled "Fitness Enhances the Quality of Your Life" and published in *Empowering Business Resources*.[20] They are:

- Eat a good breakfast
- Don't eat between meals
- Maintain your weight
- Don't smoke
- Exercise regularly and sensibly.

Sheehan suggests that the benefits of exercise are both physiological and psychological. In other words, exercise helps you reverse the effects of an inactive life-style and helps you deal with the stress of life. We agree. There's nothing like exercise to release the tension, even if it is something as unglamorous as cleaning the attic.

In addition to these tips, we recommend that you investigate and implement other activities to manage your stress and balance your life. Marjorie Blanchard, Ph.D., has developed a model for maintaining a balanced life. The model, described by the acronym PACT, outlines four areas that effect a feeling of balance and reduce stress. She encourages people to work on the following areas in her essay entitled "Make a PACT to Balance Your Life," published in *Empowering Business Resources*:

- Perspective—the ability to take a "big picture" view of the events surrounding you.
- Autonomy—the feeling of individual control of events and outcomes.

[20]Scott, Foresman and Company, 1990.

- Connectedness—the quality of your relationships and a feeling of contentment with your physical environment.
- Tone—how you feel about yourself physically.

Today's leaders must have physical stamina to compete in a global marketplace. The increased stamina will result in increased productivity, a more energetic leadership style, less stress, and longer life.

A lady of our acquaintance bought a home in a small, rural Texas town when she turned sixty, thinking she would live out her last few years in the town where she grew up. Now one hundred years of age, she is still there, living alone and in excellent health. (In fact, she still does all her own yard work.) Marc asked her, "Are you glad you moved here thirty-nine years ago?" She immediately snapped, "No! If I'd know I was going to live this long, I'd have moved somewhere more exciting where I didn't have to work so hard!" Little did she know a low-stress rural environment and undertaking all her own yard work probably contributed to these added years.

MENTALLY AWAKE

Baden-Powell drew on his experiences from childhood and as commander of an army scout unit when creating the Scouting program. He knew that a scout must be mentally awake or the enemy might slip through the line of defense, or he might miss some vital information.

Though the physical dangers facing us today are not the same, they do exist. With the rise in crime and terrorism, we must always be "mentally awake" as we go about our lives. Today's leaders must also be mentally awake to what's going on in their organization, their marketplace, and the world if they are to compete and lead effectively. In today's world that means being mentally awake to change. To be effective, the leader must be mentally awake to:

- Changing needs of the organization
- Changing needs of individuals within the organization
- Changing needs of customers
- Changing needs of suppliers
- Changing needs of the communities in which they operate
- Changes in technology
- Changes in the actions and behavior of their competitors.

Our world is exploding with change, and as we mentioned in Chapter Three the seven last words of any organization are "We've never done it this way before." Tradition is a fine heritage, but a lousy excuse for missing any opportunity to improve.

Staying mentally awake to opportunities and challenges requires you to be willing to look at and seek new information. That means we must be open to change. Most people are in favor of change as long as it doesn't affect them. In our work with organizations and their leaders, we hear many people saying that a change is needed. Most, however, believe that the change should begin with someone else. The typical response is "I am doing things the right way now!" or "I am open to new possibilities, it's the other people who refuse to change." The truth is, change is usually difficult for everyone. Even positive change brings on anxious feelings. But the alternative to change and adaptation is to die. In other words, you must be mentally awake to growth and development or you and your organization will stagnate and perish. Effective leaders accept change as the only way to grow and flourish. They stay mentally awake to embrace change that results in improvement. They continually seek information that they can use for a competitive advantage.

One way to stay mentally awake to opportunities is to read. Effective leaders read newspapers, journals, magazines, newsletters, books, and anything they can get their hands on to gather information. We know many leaders who regularly read four newspapers every day and several who read as many as seven. To accomplish this task, they read only those sections that will provide them with information they can use. Individuals who believe they don't have time to read the books necessary to stay current in their field might consider subscribing to book summaries or listening to audiocassettes. It's important to remember that staying mentally awake is more than keeping up with the latest business developments. The effective leader also spends time on personal development. She knows that self-improvement increases willingness and ability to change.

Ed Foreman was a millionaire by the age of twenty-six and is the only person in the twentieth century to be elected to Congress from two states (Texas and New Mexico). Today, he helps individuals grow and develop through a three-day program called The Successful Life Course. Ed believes that individuals should feed their minds properly if they hope to prepare themselves for success. He recommends:

- Daily reading of inspirational books
- Regularly listening to positive messages
- Associating with positive people
- Thinking about what you want to have happen.

Another way to monitor change is to listen—to customers, employees, peers, suppliers, competitors—anyone. Listening is the most used form of communication and the communication skill least developed. All of us hear, but few really listen. Listening requires us to focus on the message given by the other person or group rather than on the message we want to give. Often, we spend the time when others are speaking thinking about what we want to say next rather than using the opportunity to listen. Corrie ten Boom, author of the best-selling book *The Hiding Place*,[21] related an incident from her childhood when she was introduced to an elderly woman. A moment later, Corrie confessed, "I'm sorry, but I've forgotten your name." The elderly woman smiled and said, "That's all right, dear. When someone is introduced the only name they ever hear is their own."

The first goal of communication is to hear. The second is to listen. Only when we have done this have we earned the right to be heard and listened to. Effective leadership involves constant two-way communication. The leader uses information gleaned from the organization, its customers, suppliers, and the community it serves to look for new opportunities, stay alert for challenges that might affect success, and keep the organization on track. The leader then uses the information to communicate the organization's direction. Stephen Covey, Ph.D., provides a wonderful illustration of the difference between leadership and management in his book *The Seven Habits of Highly Effective People*.[22] Covey asks his readers to imagine a group of producers moving through the jungle. The producers are the

[21]Fleming H. Revell Company, 1971.
[22]Simon & Schuster, 1989.

people doing the work, clearing the jungle with machetes. There are also people responsible for managing the people doing the work. These managers make sure that the work is done properly. They write the procedures and develop the programs to see that the producers are both effective and efficient. There is also a leader on this journey. The leader is the person who climbs a tree now and then to look out over the jungle and make sure the group is in the right jungle. The leader must be mentally awake to the need for change and listen to the information received if the organization is to arrive at its destination.

MORALLY STRAIGHT

Being morally straight keeps the leader moving in a direction that is consistent with society's values. Notice that the consistency is with *values* not laws. Some laws exist that many in society consider at odds with values. The morally straight leader is aware of this and keeps the spirit of the agreement as well as the letter. He or she goes out of the way to maintain feelings of fairness with everyone. Most important, the morally straight leader rarely talks about morality (remember the Emerson quote in Chapter 2 about the spoons?), choosing to *live* his moral code and demonstrate his beliefs by *action*. The moral leader deals with people quietly, on an individual basis rather than publicly, realizing not everyone has grown to the same state of moral awareness.

It is our belief that the successful leader of the future must, above all else, be morally straight. Society has come to demand that of its leaders in all walks of life. There have always been public officials and personalities who display poor judgment, but public awareness of this has increased. Industrial accidents that damaged the environment occurred before oil spills, and shady business deals were being done before the current savings and loan crisis. In many ways the media, with its ability to draw attention to individual incidents on the other side of the world and bring them into our living rooms in Technicolor, have created an environment where being morally straight is vital to a leader's survival. On the other hand, the public has a tendency to be forgiving and has a short memory when the guilty party readily confesses to the transgression. Two confessions and a question can help any leader get back on track when the moral compass strays off course:

- I did it.
- I'm sorry.
- How can I make it right?

MORAL STRAIGHTNESS IN A CHANGING WORLD

The world has changed since the writing of the Boy Scout Oath. There are fewer rivers to be explored and lands to be developed. But today, as then, we still need leaders who are physically strong, mentally awake, and morally straight. In fact, we need them more today than ever before. Our world is more complex, despite all the technological advances that have made it more convenient. Change is the order of the day. Success and survival depend on being capable of meeting the challenge.

"ON MY HONOR, I WILL"

In the spaces below, list the actions you will take to honor your commitment to become physically strong, mentally awake, and morally straight.

- _____
  _____
  _____

- _____
  _____
  _____

- _____
  _____
  _____

- _____
  _____
  _____

- _____
  _____

CHAPTER NINE

LIVING THE OATH—
LIFE-STYLE INTEGRITY

By now, the Scout Oath is familiar to us all:

On my honor, I will do my best:
1. *To do my duty to God and my country, and to obey the Scout Law;*
2. *To help other people at all times;*
3. *To keep myself physically strong, mentally awake, and morally straight.*

The Scout Oath and Law have provided direction to more than 83 million American boys. Since we learn our core values at an early age, it is safe to assume that most of those who received Scout training continue to practice the principles of integrity they learned in Scouting. Add to the 83 million Boy Scouts all those who were Girl Scouts, graduates of religious training programs, or raised by parents who valued honesty, ethics, and integrity, and you have a solid base on which to build a business, a community, a country, and a world. Most of us grew up knowing the difference between right and wrong, and the importance of integrity. Most of us consciously avoid violating our values in the important areas of our lives. We don't commit murder, robbery, rape, treason, or any of the major sins.

The moral crises most of us face are not major but what some would consider "minor." Yet any deviation from the basic tenets of honor and integrity has potentially catastrophic consequences. As the Song of Solomon says, "It's the little foxes that spoil the vines," and even small leaks, left unchecked, can sink great ships. A slight overcharge on a customer's bill, a small lie to a co-worker, a broken promise to a supplier, failure to report it when we are undercharged for an item, a missed opportunity to help build our community—little things in the grand scheme of life, but they are corrosive to our image as leaders of integrity.

The leaders we have profiled know the value of maintaining integrity with their customers, employees, shareholders, suppliers, and community—*at all levels and at all times*. They echo this statement from John Antioco, chief operating officer at Pearle, Inc.

No business or business person can be successful long-term without integrity or concern for people. Trust by employees and customers is essential for success. People respect the truth whether it is bad news or good news. Once a company loses the confidence of its employees or customers, it is the beginning of the end. A company exists to serve its customers and reward its employees and stockholders—profits merely allow the company to continue to exist.

Since the truths Antioco spoke of are self-evident, why do we continue to have problems in America? Why is there a lack of trust for leaders in politics, business, and even religion? Is it the short-term focus forced on business today by restless stockholders? Is it increased competitiveness? Is it that employers are treating employees as second-class citizens while asking them to provide first-class treatment to customers? Is it that we are conditioned for immediate gratification and are willing to do whatever it takes to get what we want now? All of these excuses have been given by those who transgress the standards of integrity. Yet "good excuses" never compensate for good behavior, and we are judged by *what we do*—not by *what we say*.

Whatever excuses others find for lack of integrity, you, as a leader with integrity, must walk as you talk. More than that, you must teach others to do the same by creating an environment of integrity and trust in your workplace. Nobody has promised that it will be easy—nothing worthwhile ever is. Building integrity in your workplace takes time, patience, persistence and—most of all—commitment.

JCPenney Company, Inc., is one company that has a long history of operating with integrity. We mentioned them briefly in Chapter 1, but let's take a closer look at how they began and how they literally became "a company built on integrity."

Case Study: JCPenney Company, Inc.

On April 14, 1902, twenty-six-year-old James Cash Penney, Thomas M. Callahan, and William Guy Johnson opened the first Golden Rule Store in Kemmerer, Wyoming. Over the next several years, as the store prospered, they set up other Golden Rule Stores, each operated as a partnership that enabled those responsible for the store's success to share in the profits.

In 1913, when the Golden Rule Stores were incorporated as the JCPenney Company, James Penney met with the partners in the Golden Rule to discuss the new company. He wanted to make certain their new organization had the same motivation, spirit, and ethical foundation that had made the company successful. The thirty-six men at that meeting adopted a company motto built on four words: Honor, Confidence, Service, Cooperation. This motto was later abbreviated to H.C.S.C. and used in the company emblem. That meeting also produced the "Penney Idea," seven principles that guide the company to this day. They are:

1. To serve the public, as nearly as we can, to its complete satisfaction.
2. To expect for the service we render a fair remuneration and not all the profit the traffic will bear.
3. To do all in our power to pack the customer's dollar full of value, quality, and satisfaction.
4. To continue to train ourselves and our associates so that the service we give will be more and more intelligently performed.
5. To improve constantly the human factor in our business.
6. To reward men and women in our organization through participation in what the business produces.

7. To test our every policy, method, and act in this wise: "Does it square with what is right and just?"

Since the beginning, the JCPenney Company has operated on what retired president and CEO Earl Corder Sames calls "a certain service we owe to our community...which is merchandise at a fair profit." The result is that Penneys has become an institution in America. The company has never suffered a serious ethical crisis in its history. W. R. Howell, current chairman of the board, shared this example of the integrity that built the company in an October 1990 speech.

> Mr. Penney was on the board of directors of a bank in Florida during the Great Depression. He had nothing to do with the day-to-day running of the business, but his name and reputation were instrumental in bringing in depositors. Well, like so many other financial institutions at the time, the bank folded and there was an outcry from depositors. Many could not understand how a bank associated with Mr. Penney could fail while he remained a multimillionaire. Mr. Penney was so anguished by the event that he used a large part of his personal fortune to pay the depositors what they had lost. He clearly was under no legal obligation to do so. He simply felt it was the right thing to do. That's the kind of person he was—and that's the kind of legacy he left. He never forgot that when you're a company that serves the public, what you are and how you conduct yourself become a part of your name and reputation.

The policies and principles of integrity that Penney first formalized in 1913, which developed the "Penney Idea," are still in place today. Pins with the motto "H.C.S.C." are presented to new management associates at a formal ceremony. An affirmation ceremony is held every four or five years. Its purpose is to welcome partners into the company and reinforce the company's founding principles. According to Howell, the key ingredient in passing on the spirit of integrity is "leadership by example."

How does an organization make certain that integrity permeates the organization? James E. Oesterreicher, executive vice president and director of JCPenney stores, addresses the problem in these words:

> A company may have an ethics code that prohibits certain business practices, but the prevailing culture may say, "Do what it takes, just don't let us know about it." A company can't let down its guard for a moment...unethical behavior can arise at any time within any business."

In other words, it is up to the organization's leadership to create a high-integrity work environment that allows customers, employees, and the community to have their needs met only by embracing integrity! Robert Waterman, coauthor of *In Search of Excellence*, said in his second book, *The Renewal Factor*, that the effect of any management program pales in comparison to the effect of managers paying attention to the results they want over time. If integrity is the main thing you want in your workplace, you must make it important on a daily basis!

Companies like Penney's have the inside track in

passing on a heritage of integrity because generations of managers have worked to keep the principles alive; they are often found posted in the offices of Penney managers. The fact the principles are posted, however, isn't as important as the fact they are practiced. It is the *practice* of the principles that leads to success.

In a speech given at Texas Christian University in September 1989, Oesterreicher outlined three additional actions organizations can take to help create a high-integrity work environment:

- Communicate the organization's expectations to employees
- Hire and promote based on demonstration of high ethical standards
- Deal swiftly with unethical behavior.

To today's leaders at JCPenney, integrity is more than just good business philosophy, it is good business—period. The company continually rates high on customer surveys of honesty, integrity, fair play, and value. They are the fourth largest retailer in North America, with 196,000 full-time employees in 1,300 stores. They operate the nation's second-largest catalog business, nearly 500 Thrift Drug Stores, and several specialty boutiques. They also own the JCPenney Life Insurance Company and the JCPenney National Bank. Sales in 1989 were more than $16 billion. They have achieved these impressive results by staying true to the mission that existed in 1902, **"To sell merchandise and services to customers at a profit in a manner that is consistent with our corporate ethics and responsibilities."** In addition to the direct benefits, JCPenney gains some not-so-obvious advantages:

- They attract people who share their philosophy, so the environment gets perpetuated. They have a great number of second- and third-generation management in the company, all of whom have grown up hearing, believing, and behaving the Penney philosophy of integrity.
- They retain a high percentage of their people. There are many examples of individuals who spend their entire career with this company.
- They get people who give back to make the community a better place. Most managers are involved in the community. In addition, nonmanagement employees are honored for their contributions to the community. Each year the company confers two awards, the Golden Rule Award and the James Cash Penney Award, to employees and charities who help others.

The JCPenney Company, past and present, provides good corporate and personal role models for integrity. Their success in building integrity as a corporate lifestyle is worth emulating. They are, of course, only one of many examples. Throughout this book we have provided many other specific examples of leaders and organizations who demonstrate their integrity through action. The one common factor we've found in organizations of integrity is that people of intense personal integrity are providing leadership by example. These leaders share a common commitment to doing the right thing in their relationships with customers, suppliers, shareholders, employees, and communities.

BUILDING HIGH-INTEGRITY WORK ENVIRONMENTS

JCPenney began building a high-integrity work environment in 1902—nine years before publication of the

Scout Oath. Their executives are quick to admit that you never *arrive* at your destination because it is a continuous journey. Management must instill its commitment into each new employee and continually reinforce the management with seasoned workers. An old Chinese proverb says, "A journey of a thousand miles begins with the first step." Yet, if we are to succeed in building a high ethical base in our organization, we must make that beginning. The first step is a commitment by leaders such as you to make integrity a guiding principle for every decision. The second step is to communicate that commitment to your employees, shareholders, customers, suppliers, and the community. That communication is often by the printed and spoken word—but words mean nothing unless they are backed by deeds. We can't overstress the importance of performance. If the leadership in any organization is unwilling to practice what they preach, they would be better off remaining silent.

In our research of successful organizations, we have found high-integrity work environments are characterized by the following:

- Decisions are made on the basis of "what's right" rather than "who's right." Which decisions? All decisions. New product design, marketing, business development, employee relations, customer service, sales strategies, accounts payable schedules, contributions to charitable organizations, and everything else that comes up in the organization are subject to one standard—what is the right thing to do? We like the standard Carl Sewell uses—"How would I feel if my decision was published on the front page of the morning newspaper?"
- Expectations are clearly communicated. Employees

know what is expected in all areas of their performance, especially in the areas of integrity, quality, and service. The high-integrity organization knows that it is impossible to hold people responsible for something they cannot do or of which they are not aware.

- Lifelong growth, development, and learning are emphasized. The changing world in which we live requires us to be constantly improving if we are to remain successful. Arie de Geus, retired coordinator of group planning for Royal Dutch/Shell, has stated that "the ability to learn faster than your competitors may be the only sustainable competitive advantage." We would add that the high-integrity organization sees continual learning as the minimum required to help customers, employees, and the community meet their needs.

- There is a high degree of personal commitment. Commitment is the result of desire mixed with self-discipline. The desire comes from a support for the mission and vision. Self-discipline is the result of learning and practice. Self-disciplined individuals understand their responsibility and perform consistently to meet or exceed those responsibilities. The organization may have to institute a system of accountability to build the structure necessary for some people to learn their responsibilities. Over time, however, the imposed structure will become unnecessary as compliance gives way to self-discipline and commitment.

- Strong partnerships exist between management and employees, organization and customers, organization and suppliers, and organization and community. Partnerships are an indicator of trust. We believe trust is the primary result of integrity.

Self-Check Your Organization's Integrity Rating

Complete the assessment below to determine your organization's rating as a high-integrity work environment. Rate yourself on a scale of 1 to 5, with 5 being excellent and 1 being needs improvement.

* Decisions are made based on "what's right for all parties" and not on the basis of tradition or political positioning. _____
* People at all levels of the organization clearly understand what is expected of them in the areas of productivity, quality, service, job performance, and integrity. _____
* Individuals within the organization are continually encouraged to upgrade their skills, both technical and relationship. _____
* The organization's leaders and managers are held accountable for the development of their people. _____
* The organization's leaders set a good example of integrity. _____
* Individuals are rewarded for their performances that demonstrate integrity. _____
* The organization deals swiftly with individual performance that does not meet its standards of integrity. _____
* The organization has a reputation for honesty, value, and integrity among customers and the community. _____
* Management and nonmanagement employees are united behind the common goal of providing quality products and services to customers in a manner that communicates honesty, value, and integrity._____

- The organization acts responsibly toward the welfare of the community as a whole. _____

SCORING

If your score is forty or above, your organization does a terrific job of demonstrating its integrity. There may be a few areas you want to fine tune, but you are doing well. If you scored between thirty and forty, you're doing a good job overall, but probably there are a few specific areas on which you should work. If your organization scored below thirty, you should begin right now to make a specific effort to improve your performance. Your customers and your employees will appreciate your effort, and your organization will become more effective.

The first place to start any improvement effort is with the person you have the most ability to change—yourself. At the end of each chapter we provided you with space to list the things you would do to honor your commitment to the topic covered in the chapter. We would like for you to go back to your commitments at this point and pick the two that are most important from each chapter. When choosing your most important commitments, determine the ones that will have the biggest effect on your ability to demonstrate that principle. Then, set specific goals and an action plan to put your commitments into practice. Remember, commitment is demonstrated through *action!*

THE LURE OF EXPEDIENCE

The biggest challenge you will face in becoming a leader of integrity is the lure of expedience. Experience tells us that there are no shortcuts. But the lure of expedience tempts us to try and gain quick results at the expense of others. The leaders profiled in this book know that long-term success comes only when your commitment to succeed is founded on a solid base of integrity.

Unfortunately, many organizations talk about integrity while rewarding the lack of it. They focus on short-term profits and encourage a "whatever it takes" approach to achieving them. In this kind of environment, people who would never consider a "major infraction" of the tenets of integrity are presented with peer pressure to betray a customer, commitment, confidence, community, or conscience in order to achieve the goal.

The daily challenges to our sense of honor may appear small on the surface, but our responses over time send the true message about our integrity to those who observe us. Those who observe rightly conclude that if we are willing to sacrifice integrity for the small things, we will probably make the same sacrifice in other areas also. That is why each decision we make is important.

John Delaney and Donna Sockell, associate professors at the Columbia University School of Business, surveyed past graduates to find out about their experiences with ethics and integrity. Based on responses from 1,073 individuals, they determined that the average graduate faced 4.2 ethical dilemmas in the past year. The incidents varied from breaking the law to bending corporate policy. The most disturbing portion of their findings was that *40 percent of those who chose to act unethically were rewarded, either explicitly or implicitly, by their organization. An additional 40 percent received no feedback whatsoever from their company, while 31 percent of those who refused to act unethically were implicitly or explicitly punished!*[23] It is clear that actions speak louder than their words. It does little good to publicly praise integrity if you punish those who exhibit it and promote those who do not!

THE ETHICS LITMUS TEST

Many years ago, Dr. Harry Emerson Fodsick created a six-point test for deciding right from wrong. Dr. Preston Bradley later adapted the work, which we call the Ethics Litmus Test.

1. Does the course of action you plan to follow seem logical and reasonable? Never mind what anyone else has to say, does it make sense to you? If it does, it is probably right.
2. Does it pass the test of sportsmanship? In other words, if everyone followed the same course of action, would the results be beneficial for all?
3. Where will your plan of action lead? How will it affect others? What will it do for you?
4. Will you think well of yourself when you look back at what you've done?
5. Try to separate yourself from the problem. Pretend for a moment it is the problem of the person you most admire. Ask yourself how that person would handle it.
6. Hold up the final decision to the glaring light of publicity. Would you want your family and friends to know what you have done? The decisions we make in the hope that no one will find out are usually wrong.

[23]*Training Magazine*, September 1990.

BUILDING HIGH-INTEGRITY ORGANIZATIONS

You will rarely find the organizations profiled in this book mentioned in the media unless the subject is well-run operations with a high sense of integrity. These organizations are the places where people like to work and do business. As we have seen, the first step in building a high-integrity organization is to start with yourself. There can be no transformation in our business relationships without internal change within ourselves. No internal change without trust. No trust without integrity. But from that point forward, you will need to encourage the change in your organization. Consider the following to help you complete your task:

1. **Don't announce a new "integrity program."** This sounds strange and almost contradictory, but programs historically have both a start and a stop date. Employees often see a program as yet one more example of "management by best-seller." In addition, programs have a way of focusing on actions instead of on the desired result. Tell people why integrity is important, then prove its importance by the way you reward compliance with policy.

   If you do implement a "program" in the process of building your high-integrity organization, make sure everyone knows that the program is only a tool to help you reach a goal. It is important to keep the organization focused on the goal of becoming an organization that personifies integrity. Programs come and go, but values such as integrity, quality, and service are always there as the guiding principles of organizational and personal success.

2. **Decide how you want customers, employees, and suppliers to perceive your organization.** Commu-

nicate your expectations clearly, measure the results, and continue to make integrity important through reinforcement and accountability. There's an old saying that goes, "Results occur when you inspect what you expect." What you expect must not only be inspected, it must be respected—it must be realistic. If your company has a poor reputation among customers or suppliers, don't tell your employees you expect a complete turnaround in thirty days. Tell them what your long-term goal is and set a series of incremental goals that steadily build trust. Once you communicate your reasonable expectations, however, you have a right to expect compliance. Constant measurement, reinforcement, and accountability will send the message that integrity is important—whatever your past track record has been.

3. **Structure your organization's systems so they are consistent with your values.** Employees from many organizations have told us that their organization devotes a great deal of time and energy to making sure the customer is treated well while paying little attention to the systems that ensure quality products and services. Smiles and apologies will get you through an occasional lapse, but they won't save you over the long haul. Long-term success requires systems that ensure things get done right the first time. Each organizational system should be evaluated based on the following questions: Are we doing what we said we would do? Are we providing what we said we would provide?

You need to ask these questions about every organizational system—production, distribution, customer service, financial management, compensation, performance management, selection, marketing, sales, management information systems, engineering, etc.

A breakdown in any area will give some the excuse they need to justify their own poor performance. Support the systems with training in areas like communication, decision making, leadership, commitment and responsibility, customer service, quality, and conflict management. You not only need to support these things, you need to promote them.

4. **Promote traditions and legends regarding integrity.** JCPenney re-creates the ceremony in which James Cash Penney and the original partners pledged their commitment to the company's values. Mary Kay Cosmetics uses ceremonies to create and promote legends of service, productivity, and integrity. "Foots" Clements gives away marbles inscribed with the Golden Rule. In other words, make integrity the number one value in your organization and continually reinforce your commitment.

5. **Remember and practice the two "p's" for managing change—patience and persistence.** Change rarely occurs overnight and usually meets with resistance. The only way to reach a goal quickly is to set small goals. If operating with integrity is your big goal, create a series of small goals that will take you to where you want to be. Small goals also generate enthusiasm and show progress.

As you work to build integrity in your organization, mistakes will be made, some of them yours. Don't become discouraged! An organization free of mistakes is also free of action and learning. When the mistakes are yours, apologize quickly and publicly. When the mistakes are someone else's, confront quickly and privately.

What do you do when you meet talented, capable individuals who don't share your commitment to integrity? If that happens, it may be necessary for you to remove the individuals from the organization. When this must be done, it is important that it be done properly—remember, the integrity you exercise in this situation will be watched by everyone. Change and growth are painful, and there is always the temptation to follow the lure of expedience. There are no short-cuts to integrity—things that appear to be shortcuts are only detours that can lead you in the opposite direction.

WHAT WE FOUND WHILE WRITING THIS BOOK

Our original idea for this book was to sound a clear clarion call for a return to traditional values, for our experience in dealing with hundreds of organizations has shown us that adherence to Scoutlike principles is the only way we can successfully meet the challenging times ahead. Peter C. Browning, chairman, CEO, and president of National Gypsum Company, summed it up when he told us, "The geographical, political, and economic structures of the twentieth century are undergoing rapid alteration throughout the world. Managing such changes will be the greatest challenge facing American business during the last decade of this century. The ability to attract the right kind of leadership needed for this task will determine in large part whether we as a nation will be able to compete in this dynamic environment."

Strangely, there are some in business today who want the benefits of Scoutlike ethics without having to actually adhere to those standards themselves. It won't work. It is not enough to acquiesce to the principles mentally—you must live them.

We feel those who would try to feign honor are in

the minority. Among our own clients, we found a high percentage of successful leaders who either had been Boy Scouts or Girl Scouts, or who embraced Scoutlike ethics and integrity, and contacted them to find out the "secret" of their successes. Each person we interviewed knew or knew of others we should talk to, and the list of those we "must interview" kept growing. Every time we mentioned this project, leaders responded with the name of someone we "just had" to speak with. Far too many examples surfaced to include in a book of this length. The stories we selected, then, are merely a "core sample" and not an exhaustive list.

The bottom line is that we have learned that you *can* behave like a Boy Scout and be successful. Not only that, we have evidence from the highest echelons in business that behaving like a Boy Scout is one of the best ways to *become* successful.

Hal Johnson, managing vice president in the New York office of Korn-Ferry, one of the country's most prestigious executive search firms, echoes our belief when he told us that organizations want to know what a job candidate stands for and that he/she can be trusted. Johnson says, "A lack of integrity is often the knockout punch for candidates who are otherwise very strong."

Roger Staubach, CEO of the Staubach Company, agrees. "I can't think of a better tool for predicting the probability of a person's success in business than a measure of his integrity. If you take pride in who you are, what you do, and who you work for, your value system will be in place and you will succeed."

There will be some who will say that building integrity based on the Boy Scout Oath and Law is too simple. We understand. We are a highly technological society, and we tend to drift toward complex solutions to complex problems. Yet it is the simplicity of the

thing that makes it so effective. It is simple to memo-
rize, and once committed to memory, it becomes a
ready litmus test for integrity that can be applied on
the spot to any situation.

We can't guarantee you will be successful if you
structure your organization and your life along Scout
principles—but a lot of people have tried it and been
successful. Let's be pragmatic: any program that has
successfully taught **honor, helpfulness, fitness, mental
alertness, moral straightness, trustworthiness, loyalty,
friendliness, courtesy, kindness, obedience, cheerfulness,
thrift, bravery, cleanness,** and **reverence** to 83 million
young men must have something going for it!

We think the time for a revival of traditional standards of honor and integrity is at hand. People from
all walks of life are realizing that we are dependent
on one another for our mutual success and survival.
And, without integrity, the trust that's needed to
confront the challenges that lie ahead can never be
achieved.

It's difficult to describe how we'll know when this
book has done its job. We could measure sales—that's
certainly an indicator, but sales give us no handle on
how many put the principles into practice. We could
look for the time when organizations of all sizes operate daily from a foundation of integrity. That's a noble
goal, but we're not sure how to measure it. We could
look for the time when leaders everywhere start demonstrating their integrity through action. That is certainly presumptuous on our part to believe a single
book will have that type of effect. Maybe the best way to
know when this book has done its job is if someone
calls a person of integrity a "real Boy Scout" or a "Girl
Scout" they mean it for what it is: a sincere compliment
and a sign of respect and admiration. In his book

Presidential Anecdotes,[24] Paul F. Boller states that President Gerald R. Ford, "was 'Mr. Nice Guy.' He was, someone said, a 'Boy Scout in the White House.'" Boller went on to quote Michigan Senator Robert P. Griffin as saying, "The nicest thing about Jerry Ford, is that he just doesn't have enemies." Boller added, "Even Congressman Paul McCloskey of California, who opposed Ford on vital issues, thought well of him. 'I get tears in my eyes,' he said, 'when I think about Jerry Ford. We love him.'"

That's the kind of reaction you'll get when you operate like a "real Boy Scout" and work and live with Scout-like integrity!

There will always be detractors, those who laugh at honor and integrity and the traditional values that built our great country, our great companies, and our great organizations. But we wouldn't want to do business with any of them—would you?

The Boy Scouts of America have influenced the development of many of this country's most successful leaders. Listed here are a few successful leaders whose commitment to and roots in Scouting have been very visible.

Hank Aaron
Baseball star
John M. Belk
Chairman
Belk Store Services, Inc.
Jimmy Carter
Former U.S. president
Walt Disney
Founder
Disney Studios

Don Freeman
President
Freeman Companies
Henry Fonda
Actor
Gerald Ford
Former U.S. president
John Glenn
Astronaut
U.S. senator

[24]Penguin Books, 1981.

David Hartman
Actor
Norman Rockwell
Painter
Stephen Spielberg
Filmmaker
Willis Reed
Sports star
Mark Spitz
Sports star
James Stewart
Actor
James Lovell
Astronaut
Vice president Centel
  Corporation
Rich Little
Entertainer
Ray Robbins
Chairman
Lennox Industries
Rodney Brady
President
Bonneville Int. Corp.
John Brizendine
President
Lockheed Aeronautical
John L. Clendenim
Chairman
BellSouth
L. E. Coleman
Chairman
Lubrizol Corp.
Daniel Derbes
Retired president
Allied-Signal

John R. Donnell, Jr.
President
The Donnell Company
Hollis L. Harris
President and COO
Delta Air Lines
Harold S. Hook
Chairman
American General
  Corporation
William C. Howell
Chairman
JCPenney Company
Reuben R. Jensen
Retired exec. VP
General Motors
Richard H. Leet
Executive VP
AMOCO
Willard Marriott, Jr.
Chairman
Marriott Corporation
William C. McCord
Chairman
ENSERCH
Sanford McDonnell
Chairman emeritus
McDonnell Douglas
Walter Menninger
Psychiatrist
The Menninger
  Foundation
H. Ross Perot
Founder
Perot Systems, Inc.

J. Patrick Ross
Chairman and CEO
RAX Restaurants
Louis Sullivan, M.D.
Secretary of Health and
   Human Services
John W. Thomas, Jr.
President
Thomas Built Buses
Richard Truly
Administrator
NASA
John M. Allen
Retired VP
Reader's Digest
Thomas G. Pownall
Executive Committee
Martin Marietta
Norman Augustine
Chairman and CEO
Martin Marietta
William L. Adams
Chairman and CEO
Union Pacific Resources
   Company
Anderson Chandler
Chairman and President
Fidelity State Bank
   & Trust Company
Topeka, Kansas
Glenn A. Cox
Chairman and COO
Phillips Petroleum

Daniel W. Derbos
Retired president
Allied-Signal International,
   Inc.
James F. Gary
Chairman emeritus
Pacific Resources, Inc.
Earl G. Graves
President
Earl G. Graves, Ltd.
Robert F. Harbrant
President
Food and Allied Service
   Trades Dept.
AFL-CIO
Reuben R. Jensen
Retired exec. VP and
   director
General Motors Corp.
Edward Joullian, III
President, chairman, and
   CEO
Mustang Fuel Corp.
Charles T. Clayton
Retired president
Liberty National Life
   Insurance Company
Zenon C. R. Hansen
Retired chairman,
   president and CEO
Mack Trucks, Inc.
Evelyn T. Smith
President
Crosby Forest Products

ABOUT THE AUTHORS

Randy Pennington is a sought after speaker, workshop leader, and consultant. He regularly works with organizations and their people in the areas of integrity and commitment, and managing change. For more information, please contact:

Pennington Performance Group
4000 Winter Park Lane
Dallas, TX 75244
800-779-5295
214-980-9857

Marc Bockmon is a business communicator and writer. He has worked with over three hundred organizations in helping them effectively communicating their ideas. For more information, please contact:

Marc Bockmon
P.O. Box 7
Minneola, TX 75773–0007
903-569-3155